From A Dark Place

ROBINSON

First published in Great Britain in 2016 by Robinson
Copyright © Tony Husband and Paul Husband, 2016
1 3 5 7 9 8 6 4 2

A CIP catalogue record for this book
is available from the British Library.

ISBN: 978-1-47213-712-8 (flexiback)

Printed and bound in China by C&C Offset

Robinson
is an imprint of
Little, Brown Book Group
Carmelite House
50 Victoria Embankment
London EC4Y 0DZ

An Hachette UK Company
www.hachette.co.uk

www.littlebrown.co.uk

From A Dark Place

Tony Husband and Paul Husband

ROBINSON

Dedicated to all those who didn't make it

With love and thanks to Jeff Chandler, Linda Chelton, Emma Daggers, Emma Ferguson, Rose Latham, Tom McAlpine, Ian McMillan, Dave McCollum, Lisa Ozenbrook, Jane Riley, Marc Riley, Kirk Ryder, Jackie Scott, Alan Smith, Bill Stevens, Annie Tempest, Ruth and Pete Turner, Darren Walters, Roger Ward, Paul Wolfgang Webster, Tom Woodcock, Peter Yarwood, my friends in the Providence Project and finally Mum, Sarah, Pheobe, Daisy and our family   xxx

Foreword by Annie Tempest

First of all, I want to say how honoured I am to have been asked by Tony and Paul to write the forward to *From A Dark Place*.

I knew the difficult subject of addiction would be handled by them both with incredible gentleness, grace and honesty.

Alzheimer's, cancer, drug addiction: all life-limiting diseases. Only two of them elicit sympathy. All diseases are terrible for the sufferer and their families and loved ones. All deserve care and understanding. When my own father got Alzheimer's, I read Tony's first 'real life' book on the subject and found it so very helpful to learn about what I would be facing through his simple cartoons in a gentle, matter of fact way. In the same way, this book will bring a little understanding of how the disease of addiction progresses and how family and the Lancashire User Forum helped one addict.

In these pages, this father and son team simply tell it like it is. I know how well they have portrayed it because my own son, Freddy, was also an addict and every drawing resonated. Freddy died at eighteen years old from an overdose of heroin even after seven valiant attempts at rehabilitation. Thankfully, Paul is clean for today and is able to share his experiences with us all. There are the only two outcomes of the disease of addiction: die or get clean one day at a time. Be Freddy or be Paul. It is that stark.

Cartoonist Tony has not made stereotype characters up for this book. It is himself he is drawing; Tony Husband and his real son, Paul Husband. This is how it was. Neither of them hiding behind an invented cartoon character fearing a lobby who might whisper that he must have been a bad parent or that his son was a weak-willed layabout. It is an act of bravery on both their parts but it shouldn't have to be.

I applaud them both for the gift of this book that just might help the addict who reads it to identify and know that there IS a light if you can only find the switch to turn it on – in this case it was the LUF – and that families of addicts could do with support, not judgement.

Annie Tempest, June 2016

I was thinking about the dark times recently.
Yes, it was horrible. How did it begin, have you any idea?

I mean, you were a bright, happy, carefree little boy.

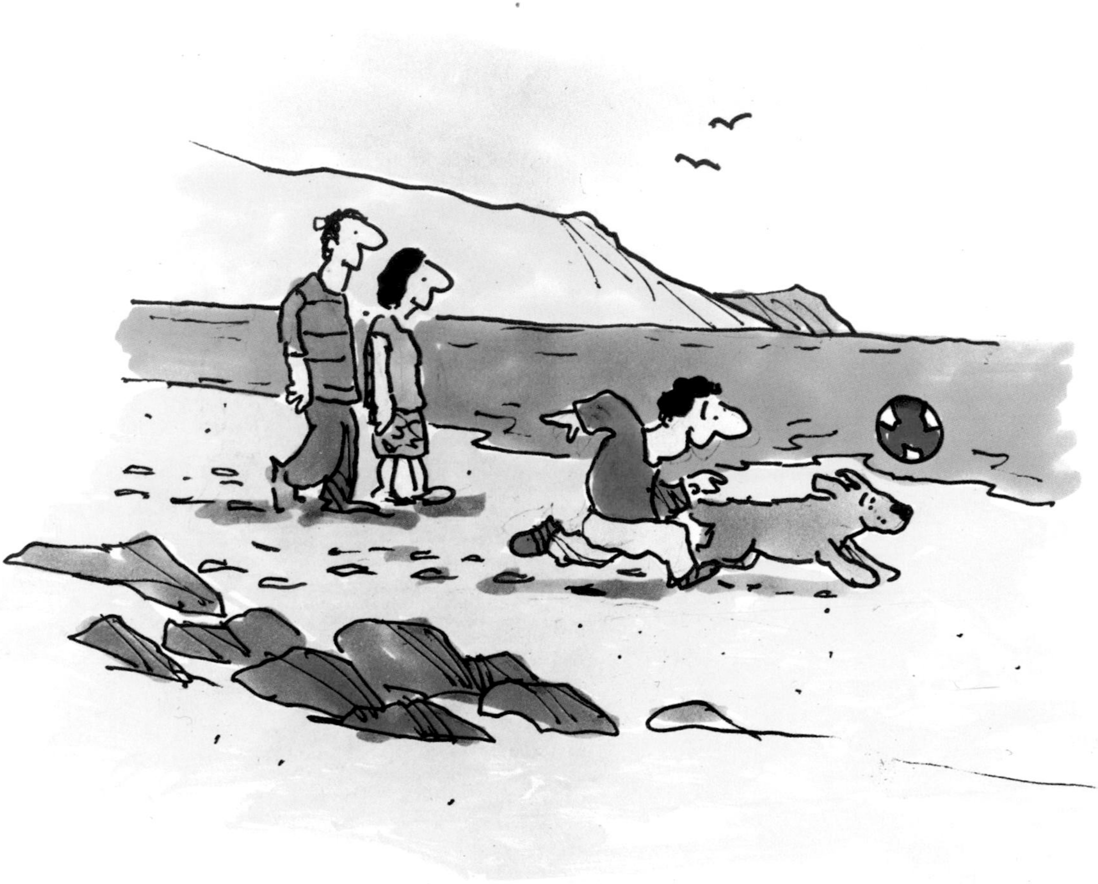

You played and loved and, let's be honest, excelled in sport.

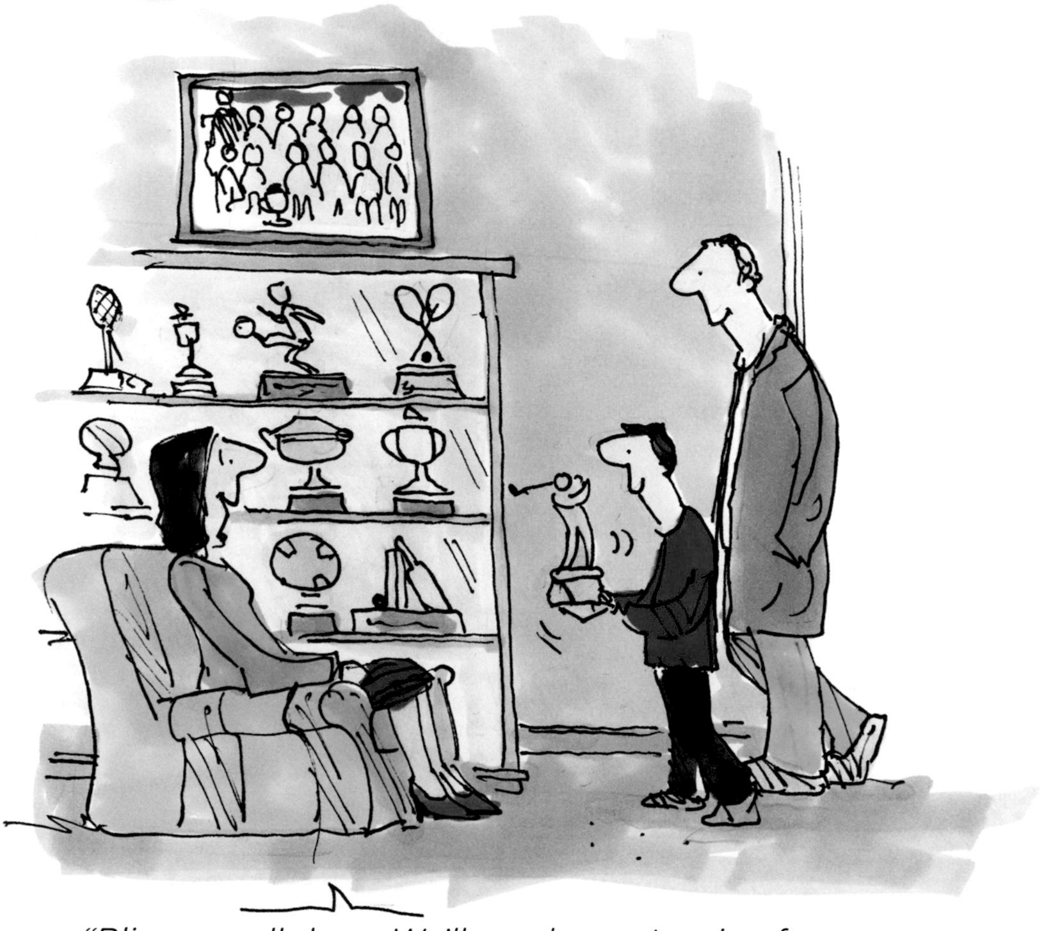

"Blimey, well done. We'll need an extension for your trophies soon!"

You loved music. You had a talent.

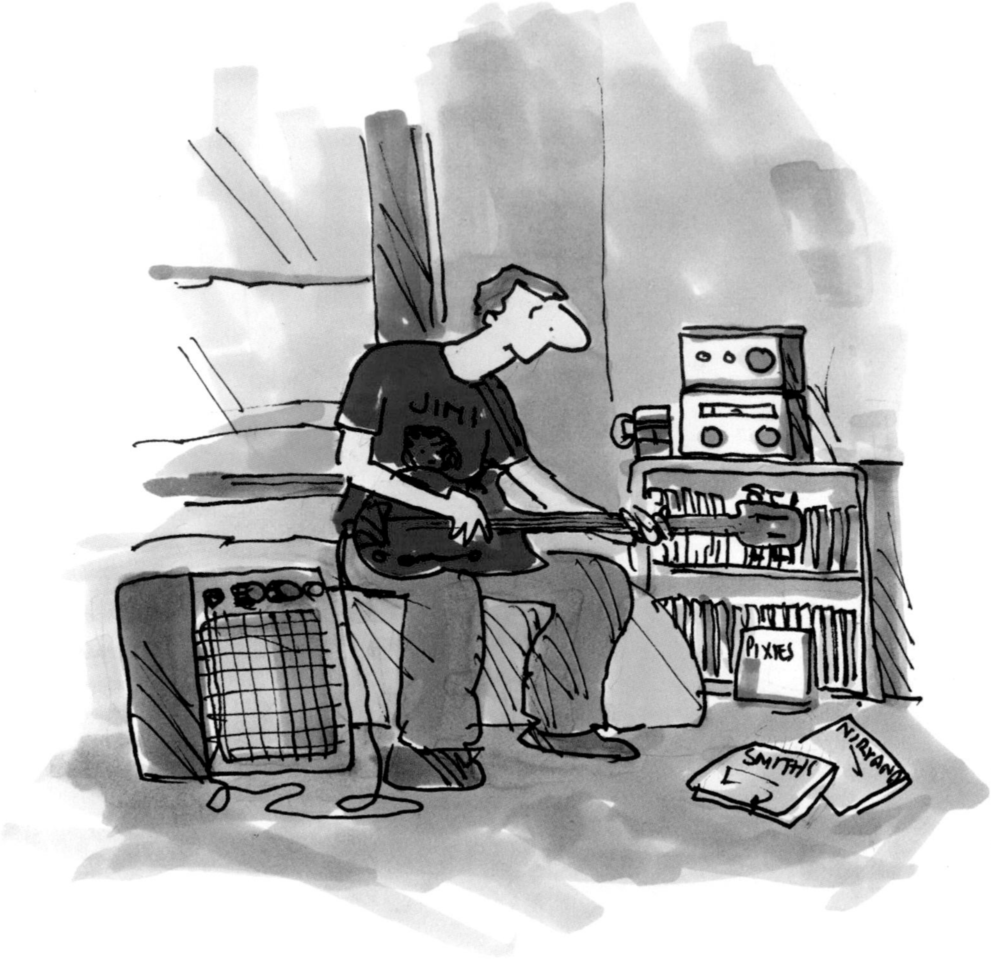
JIMI
PIXIES
SMITHS

Yes, I loved my guitars.

I think it started with the bullying. It broke my confidence, my spirit, me...

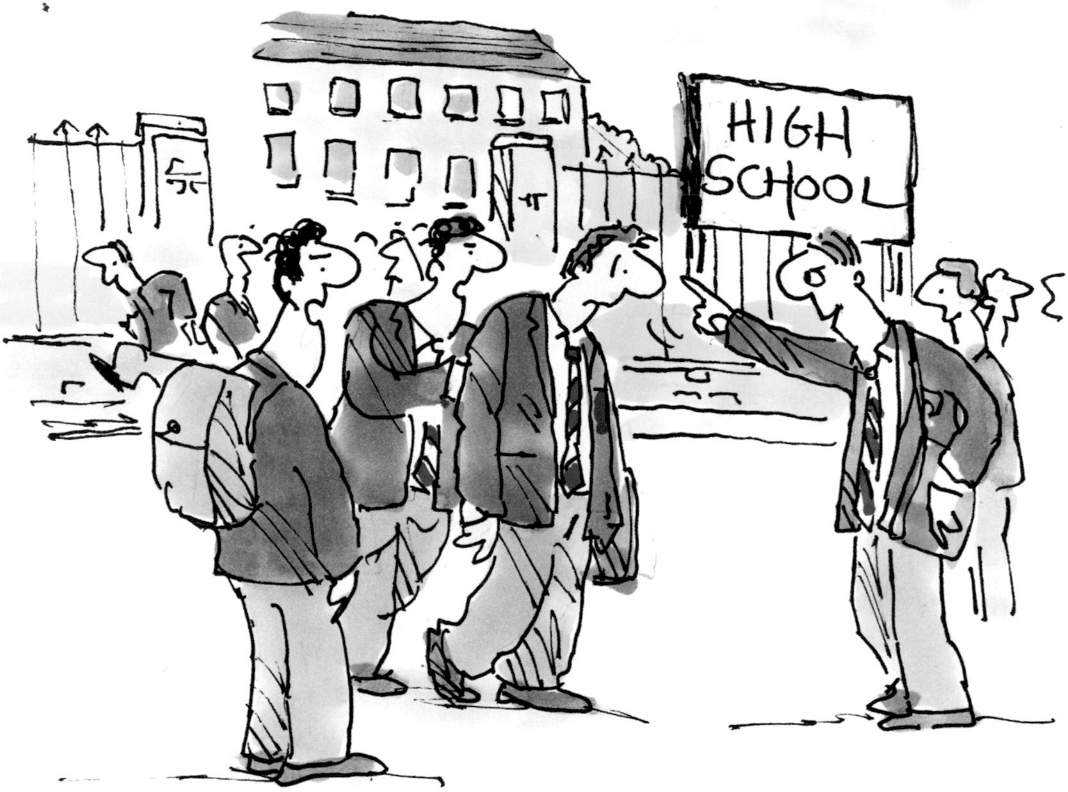
HIGH SCHOOL

That's when I started drinking and messing with drugs.
I needed to hide somewhere.

Depression, self-harming, drink, drugs... by 21
I was using heroin.

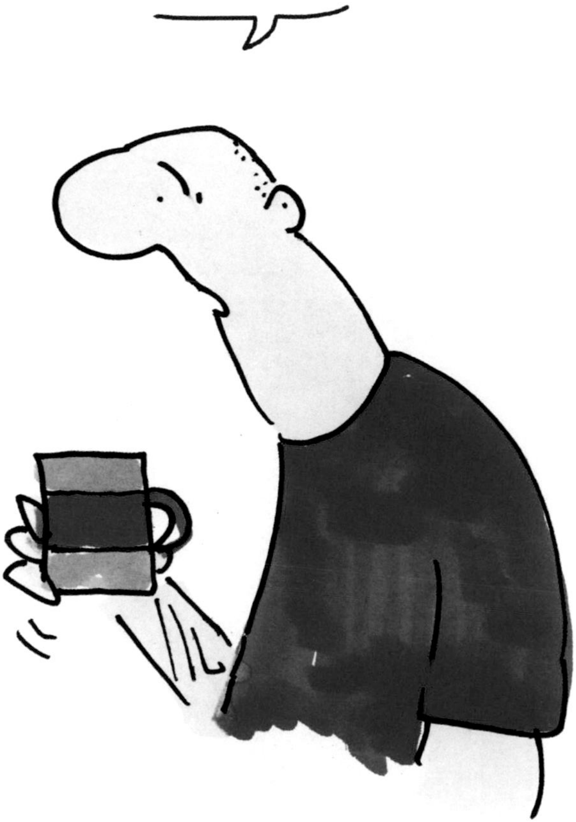

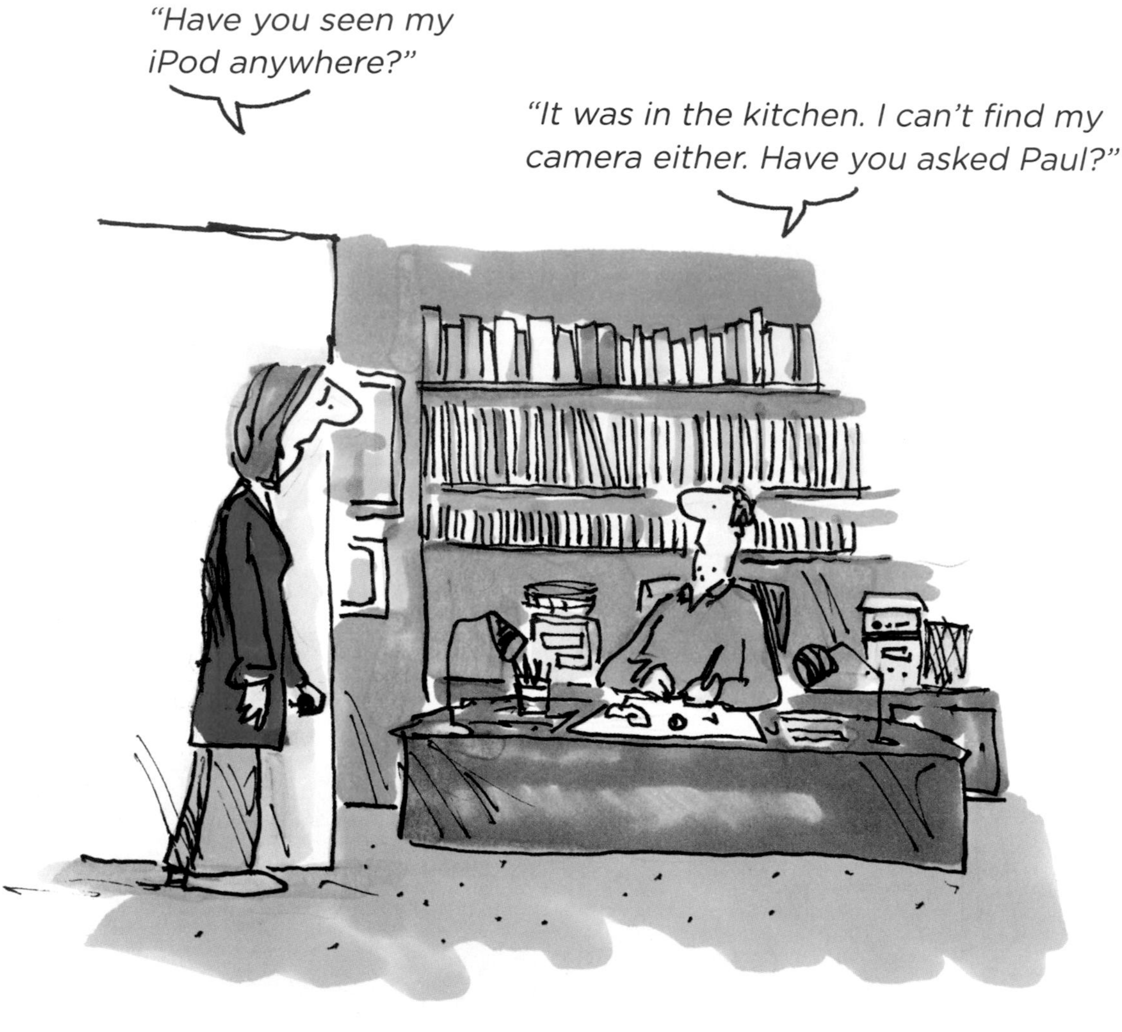
"Have you seen my iPod anywhere?"
"It was in the kitchen. I can't find my camera either. Have you asked Paul?"

"He's borrowed £20 again, too, and he's not tidied his room. It's disgusting."

"I'll go and sort out his room. I might find your iPod."

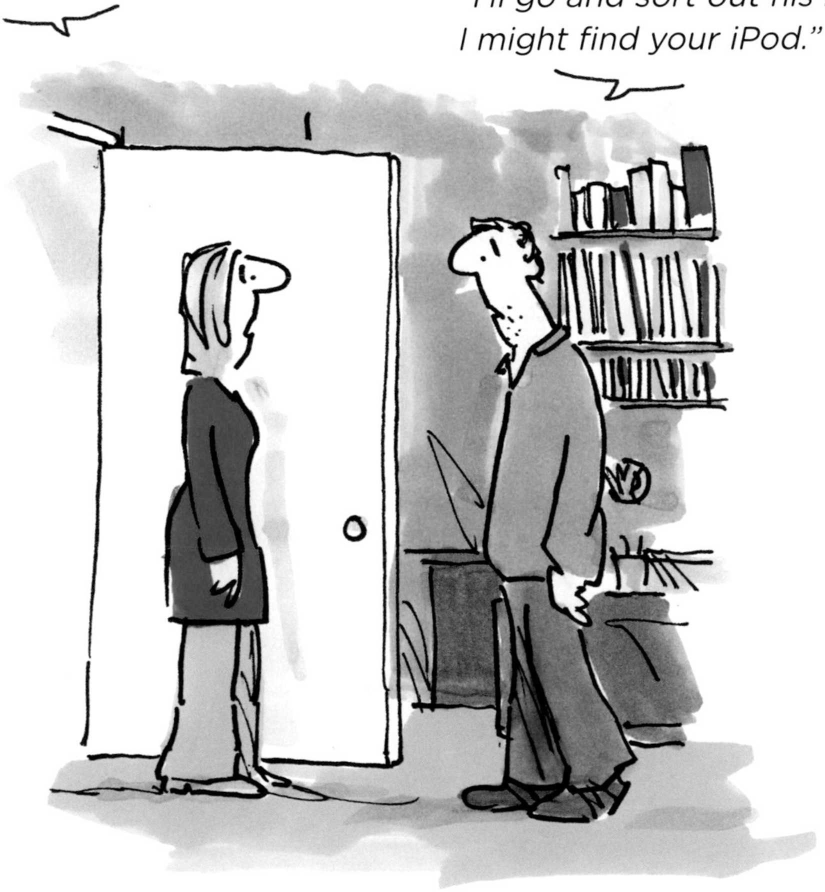

*"Christ, Paul, what a tip! What's wrong with you?
Oh no! Where are your guitars?"*

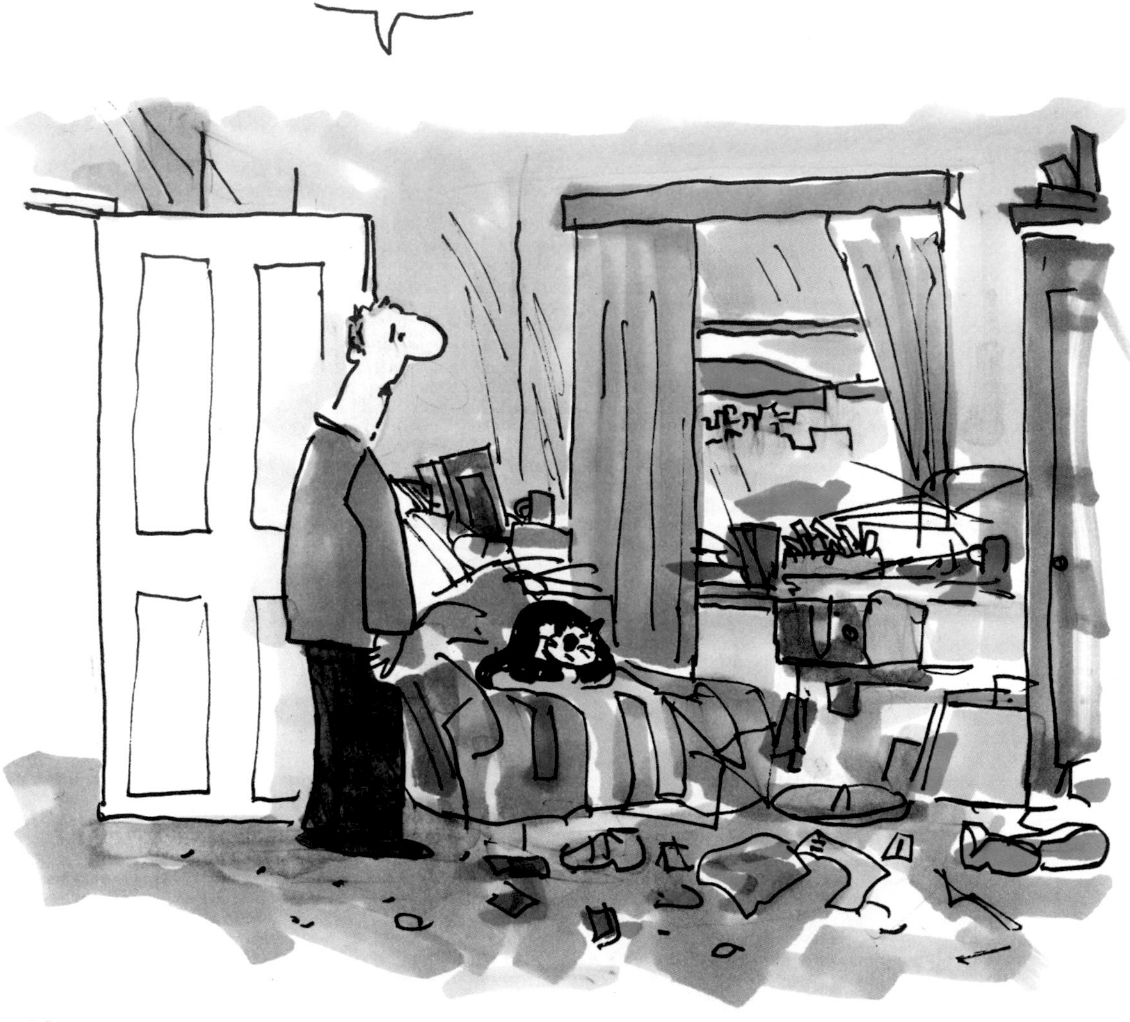

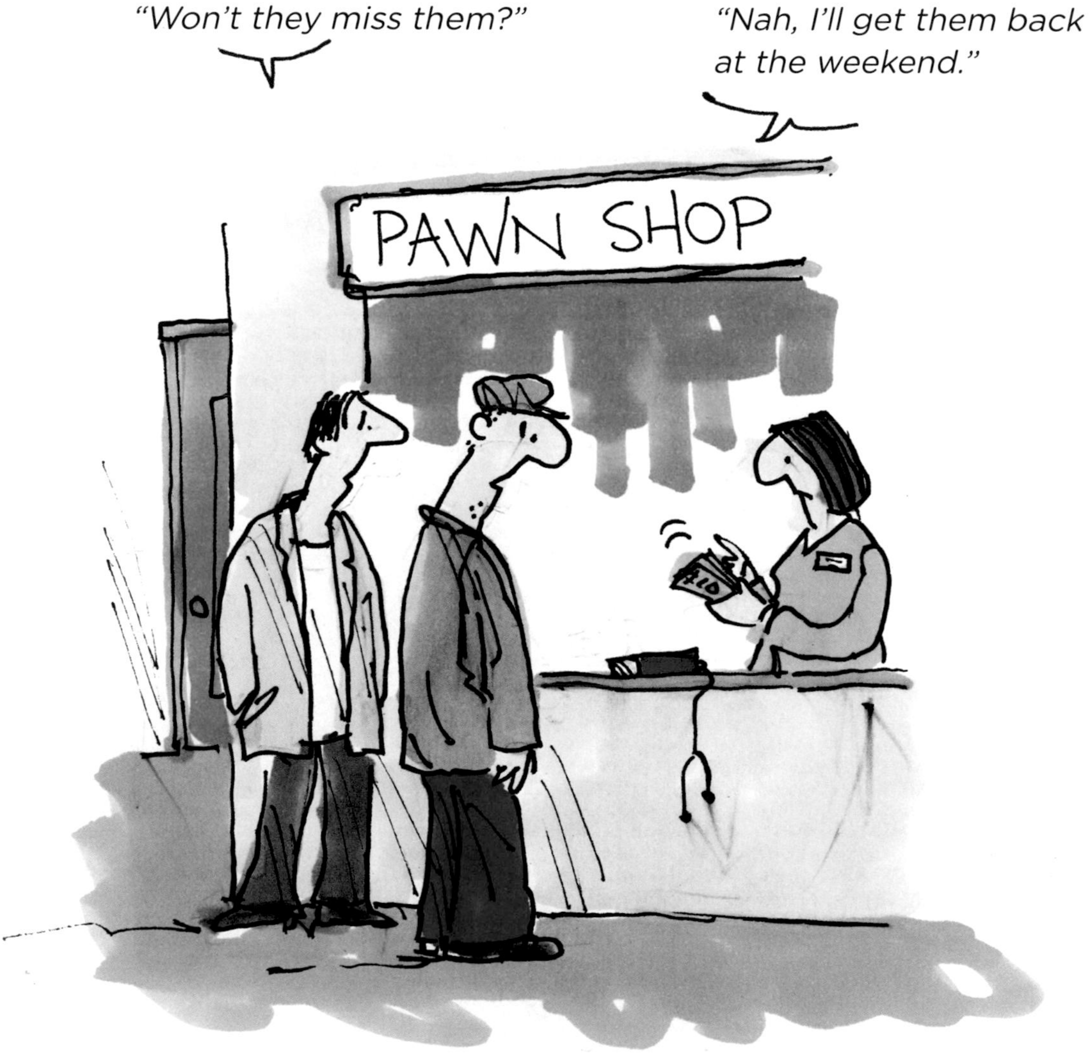
"Won't they miss them?"
"Nah, I'll get them back at the weekend."
PAWN SHOP

"Hi, it's me. Can you do me three for £25? Aye? Yes, I've got it."

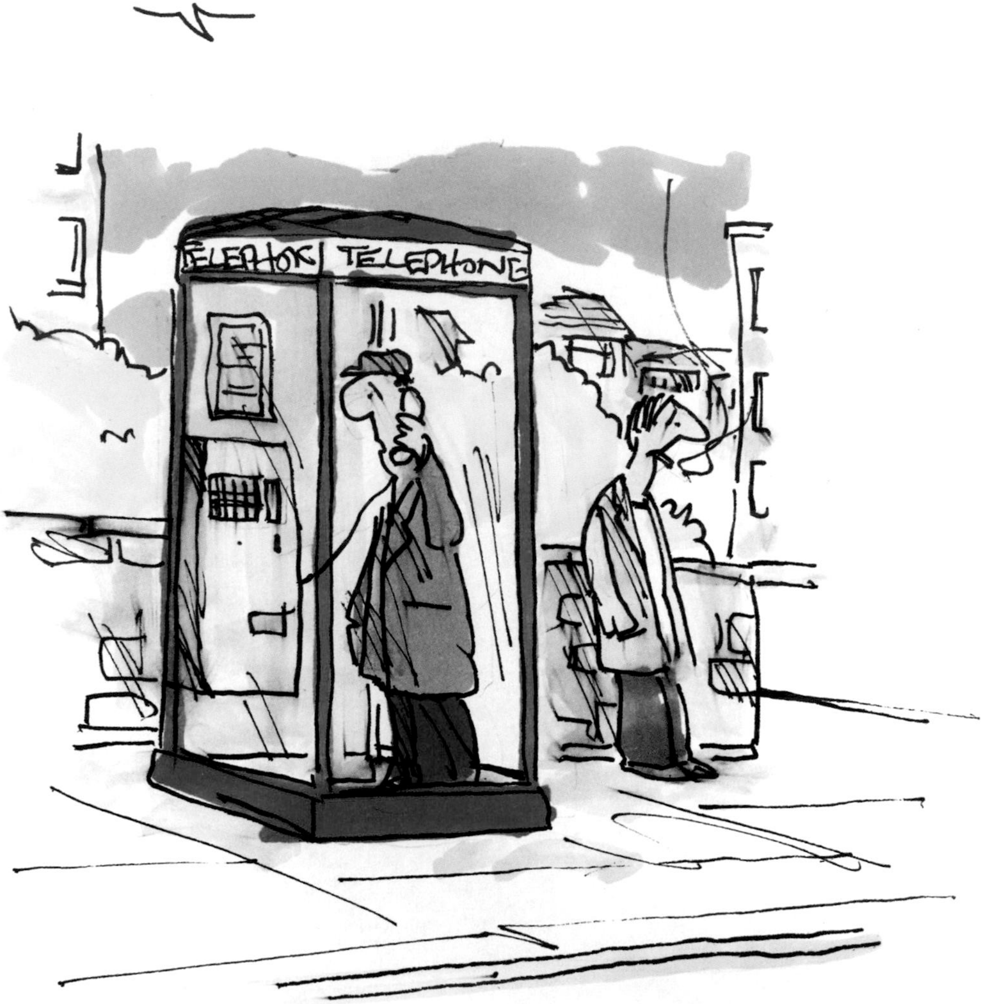
TELEPHONE

"Let's go back to mine."

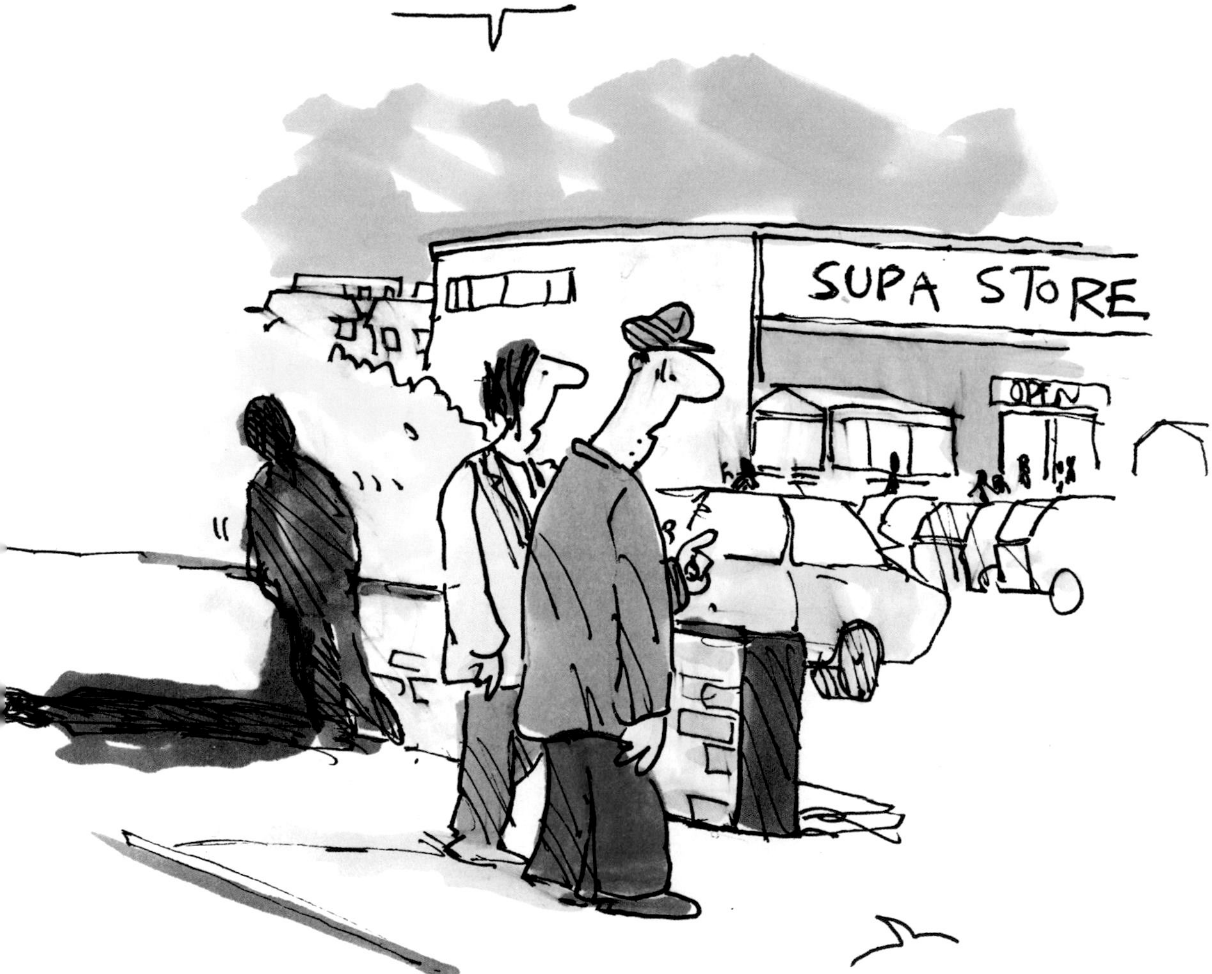
SUPA STORE
OPEN

"No, can't wait. We'll do it in here."

I'd sunk to smoking heroin in a public toilet and I never got the stuff back out from the pawn shop either. Bloody hell!

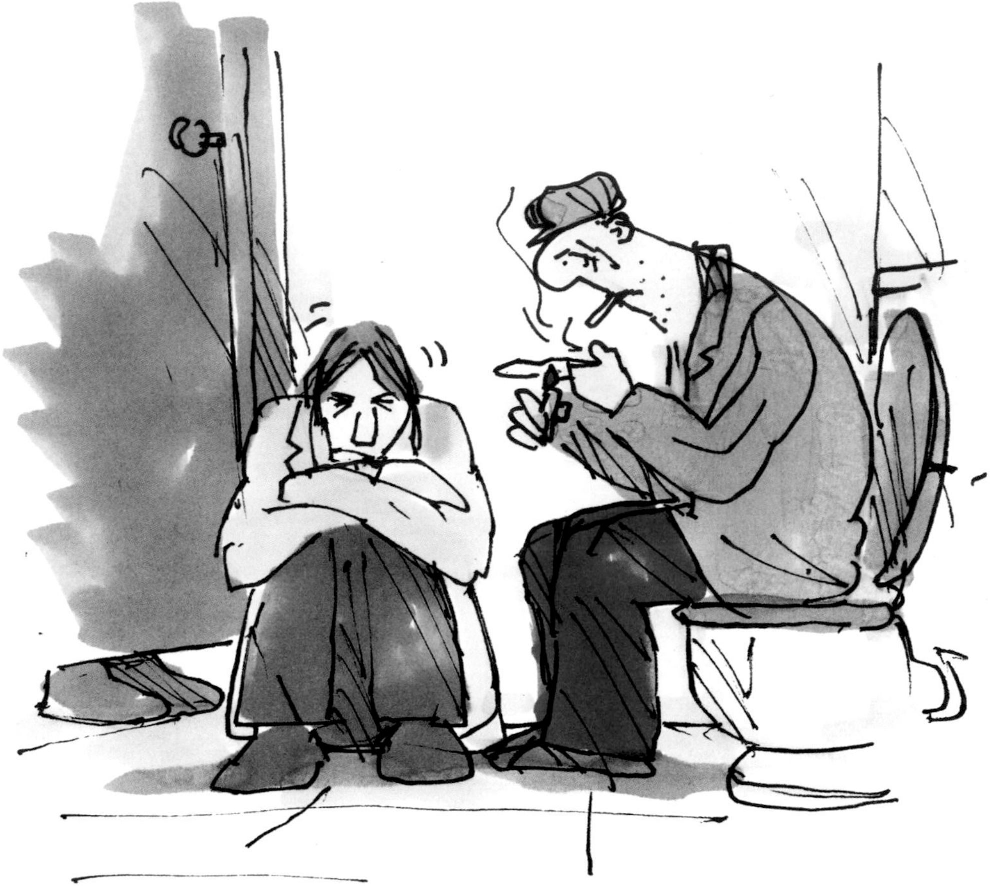

"C'mon Paul, answer your phone! ... The police, what do they want?"

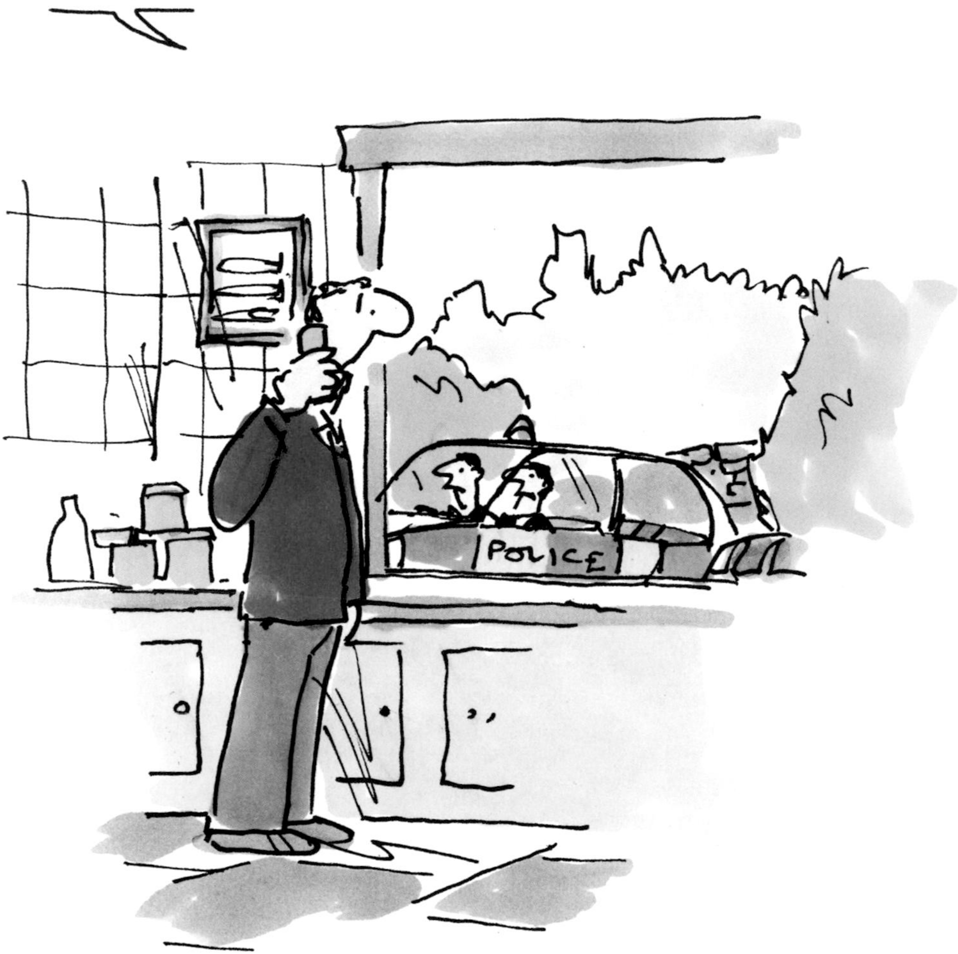
POLICE

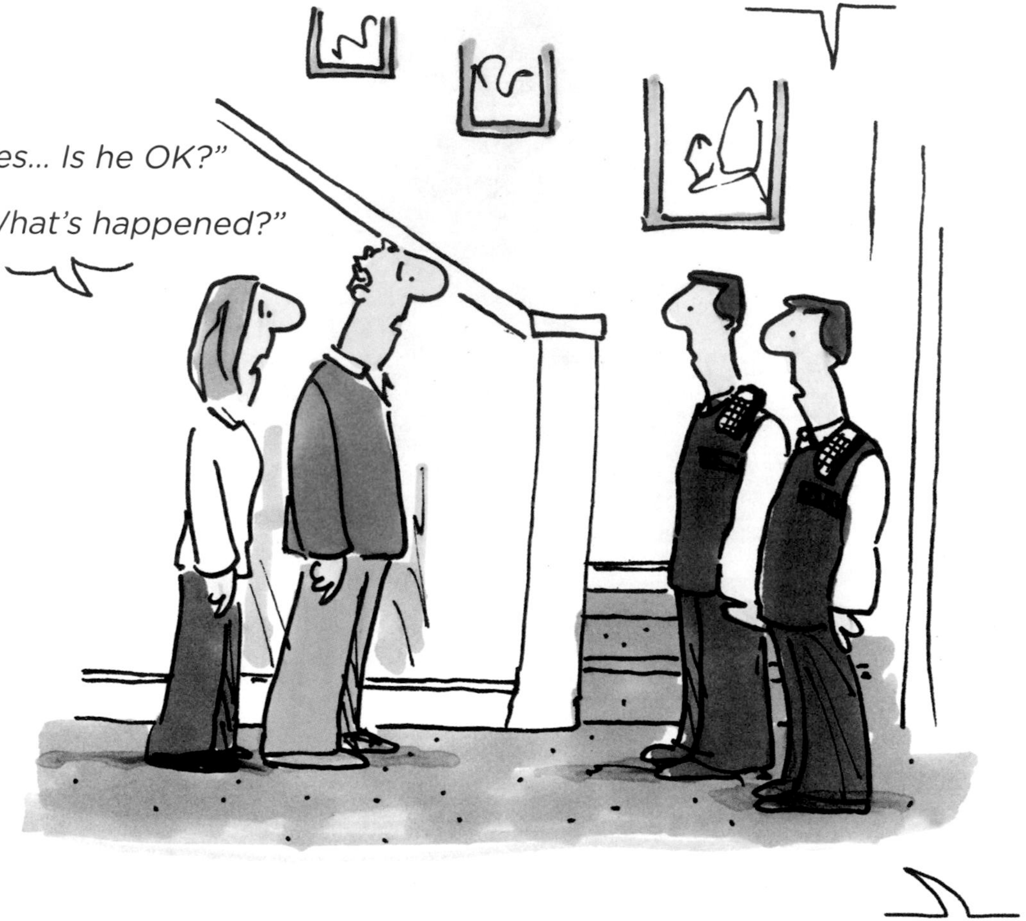
"Does a Paul Husband live here? We need to search his room."
"Yes... Is he OK?"
"What's happened?"
"He was caught using heroin in a supermarket toilet."

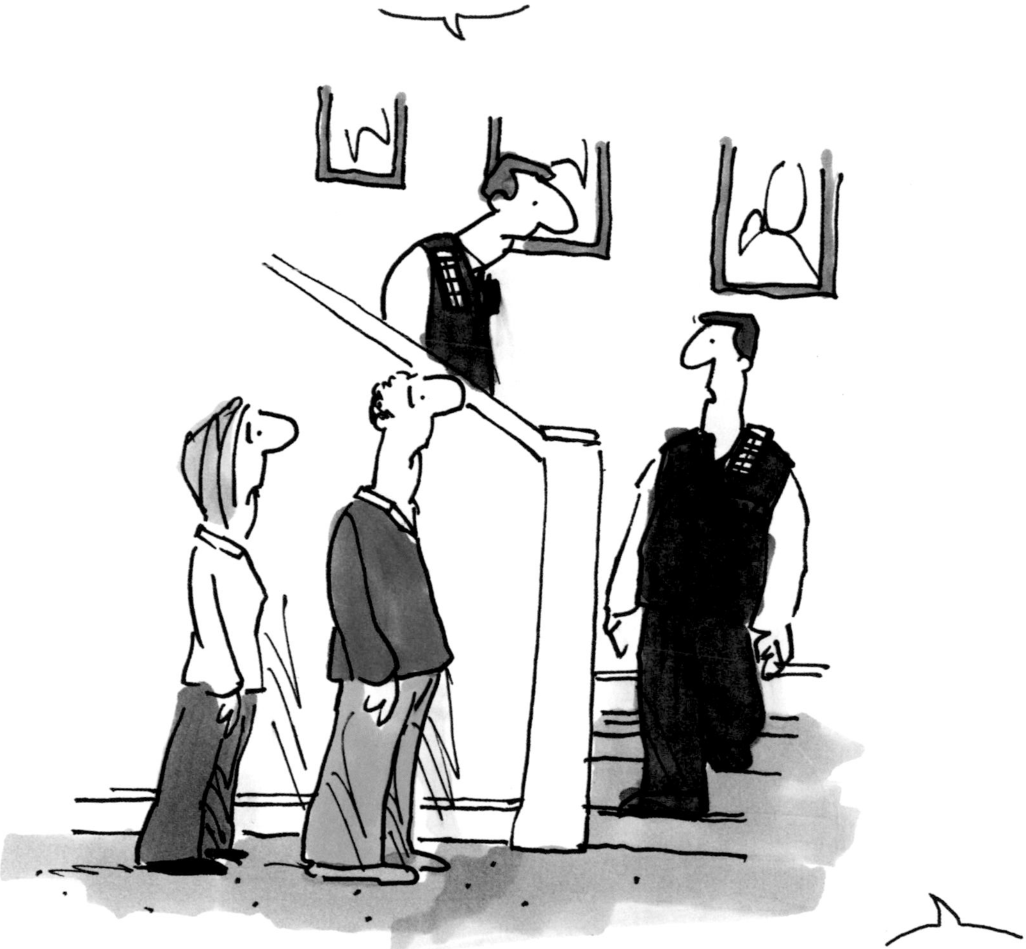
"His room's clear. We'll release him with a caution."
"He seems a good lad – genuinely upset and apologetic. It's very sad."

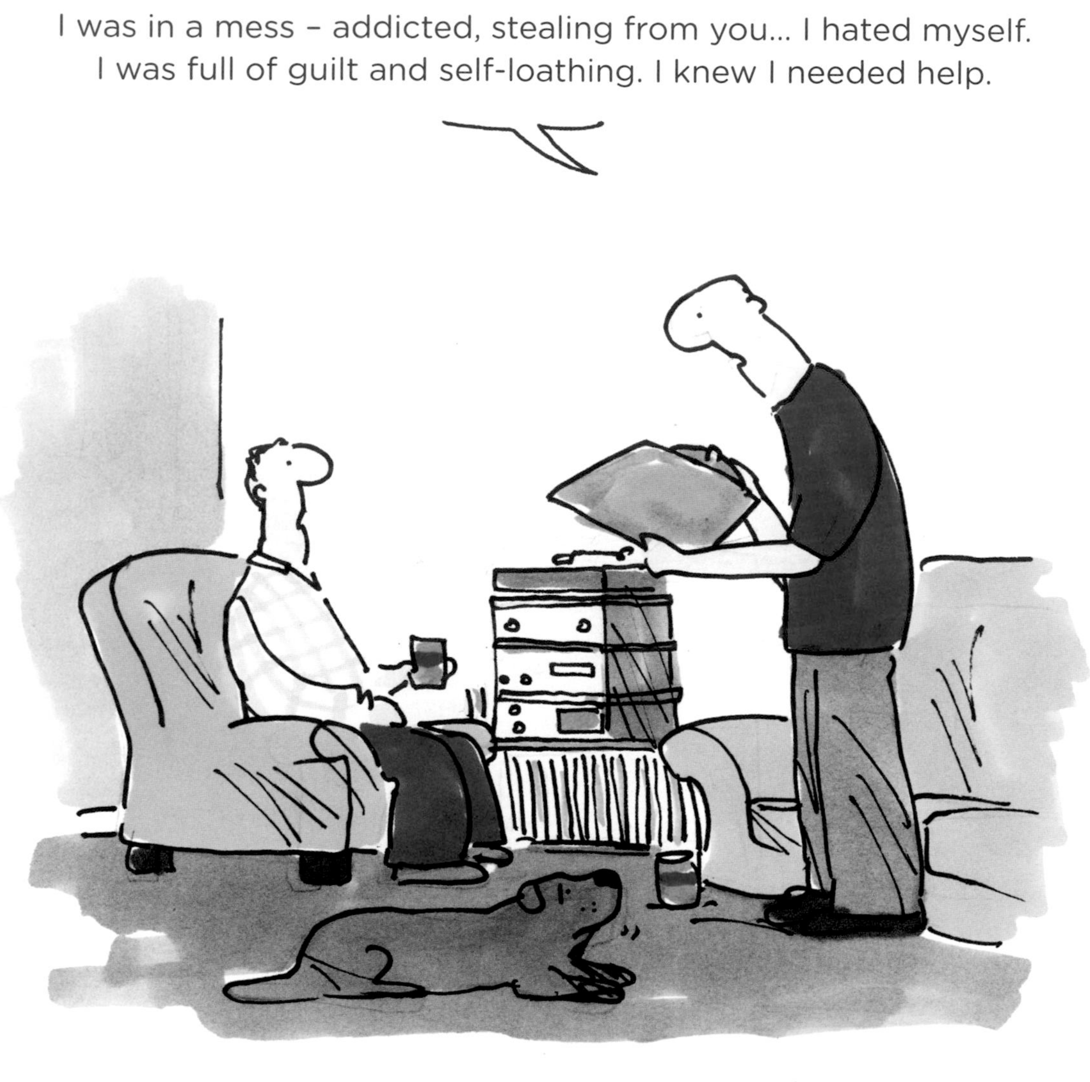
I was in a mess – addicted, stealing from you... I hated myself. I was full of guilt and self-loathing. I knew I needed help.

But help, hah! What help? Shabby, unfriendly buildings, basic treatment, no follow up, no guidance. They made us feel worthless.

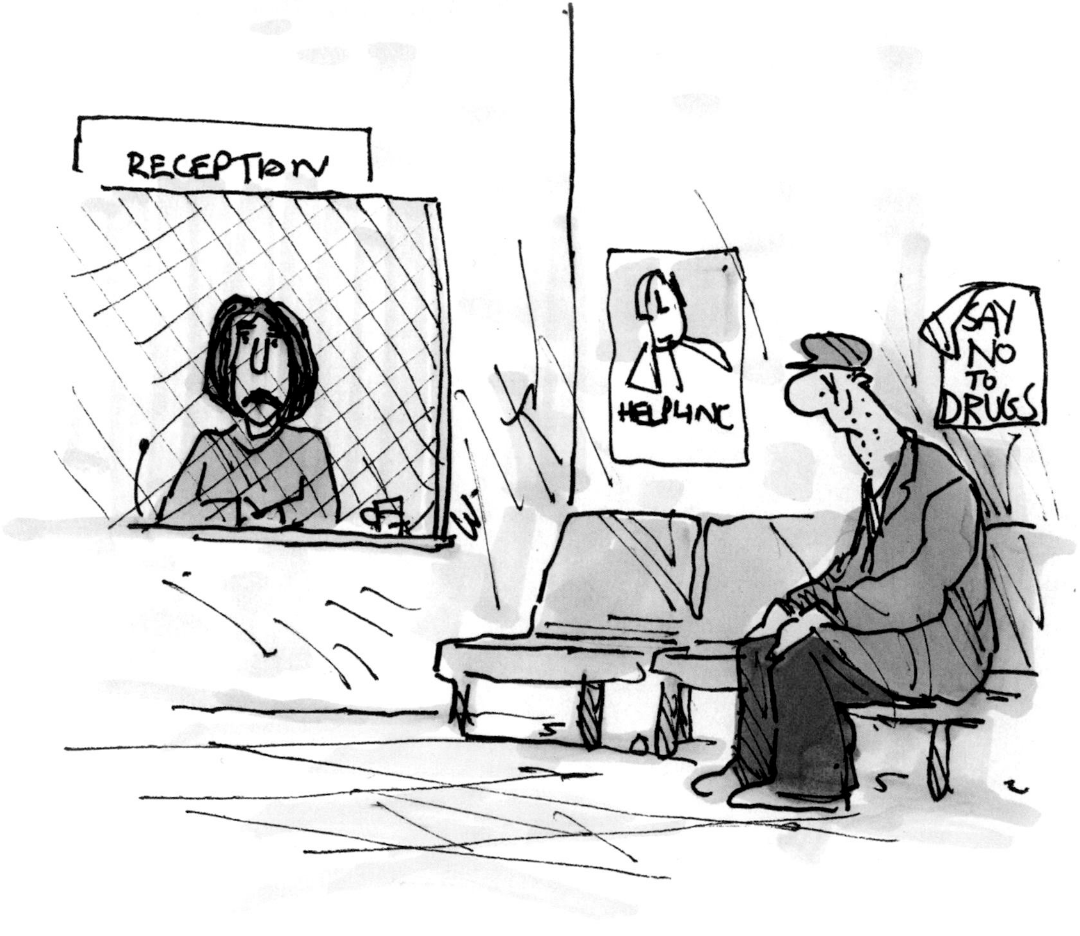
RECEPTION
HELPLINE
SAY NO TO DRUGS

All you got was a prescription.

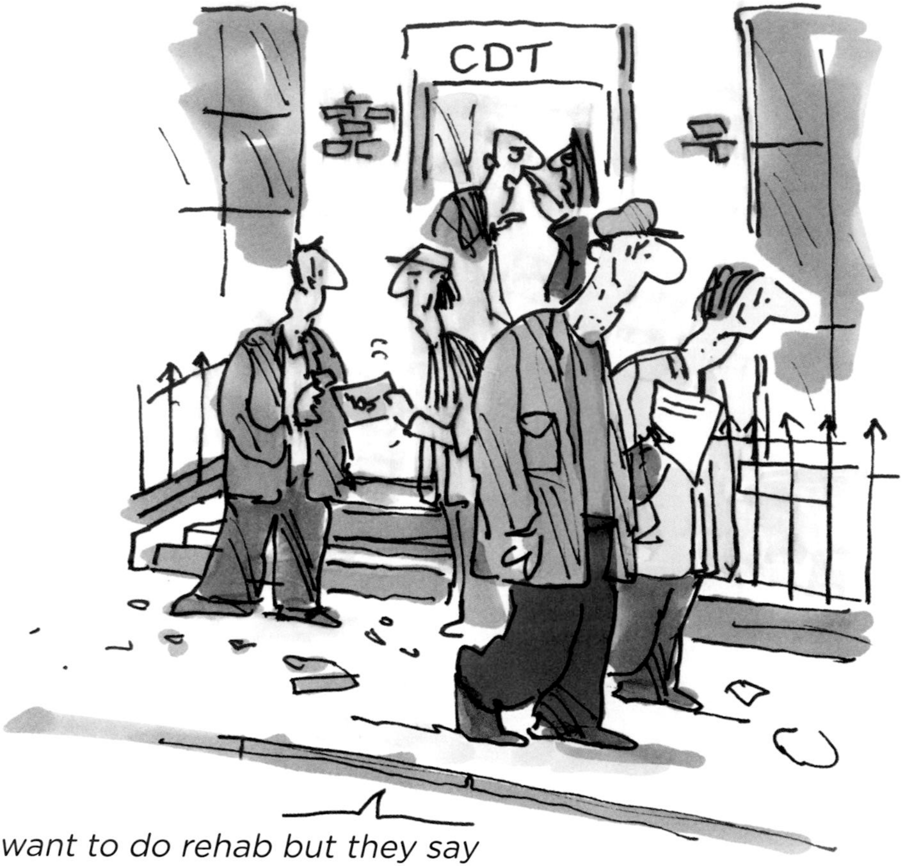
CDT

"I want to do rehab but they say I have to supply three clean samples. I'm an addict, if I could do that I wouldn't need rehab. Can we go back to yours?"

"No, I can't do this anymore... can you inject me?"
"I don't know about that Paul, are you sure?"
PIZZA

I was now injecting. I was on a terrible, slippery slope.

"Here's my prescription, and could I have some needles?"

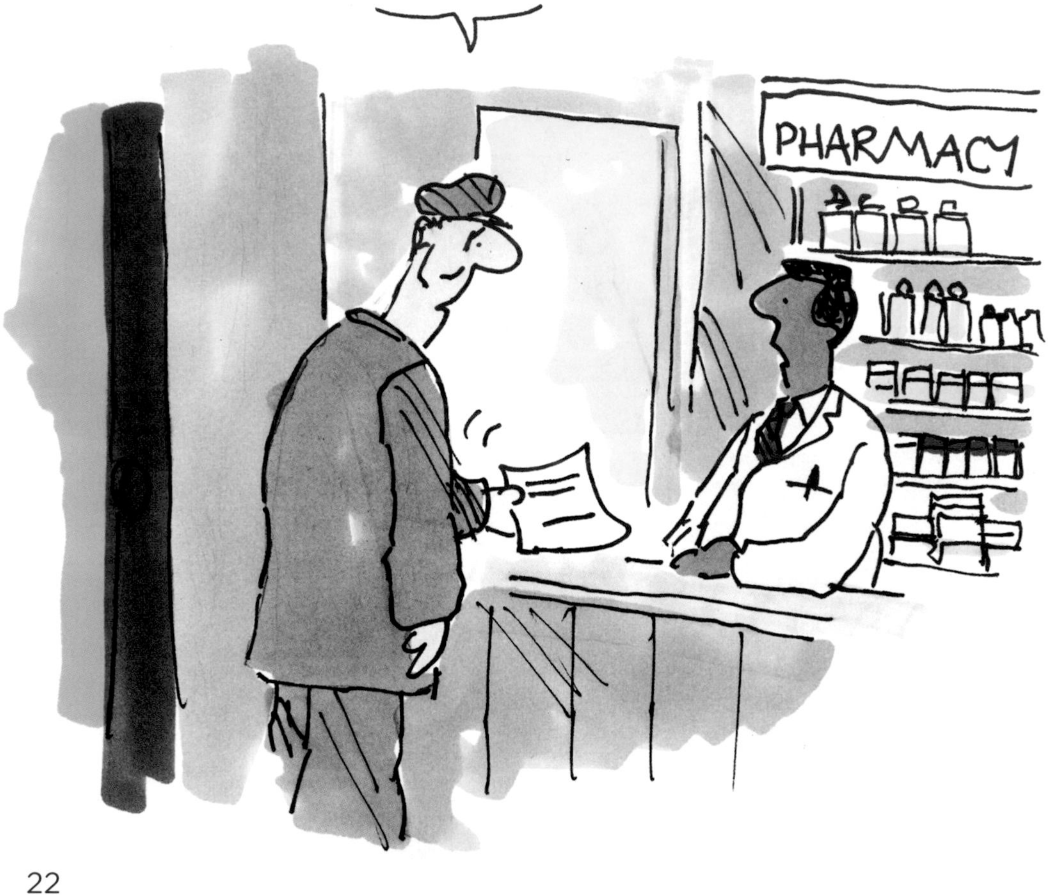
PHARMACY

I sank deeper into the addiction. It became all-consuming. I'd even begun injecting crack. I was flirting with death and I knew it.

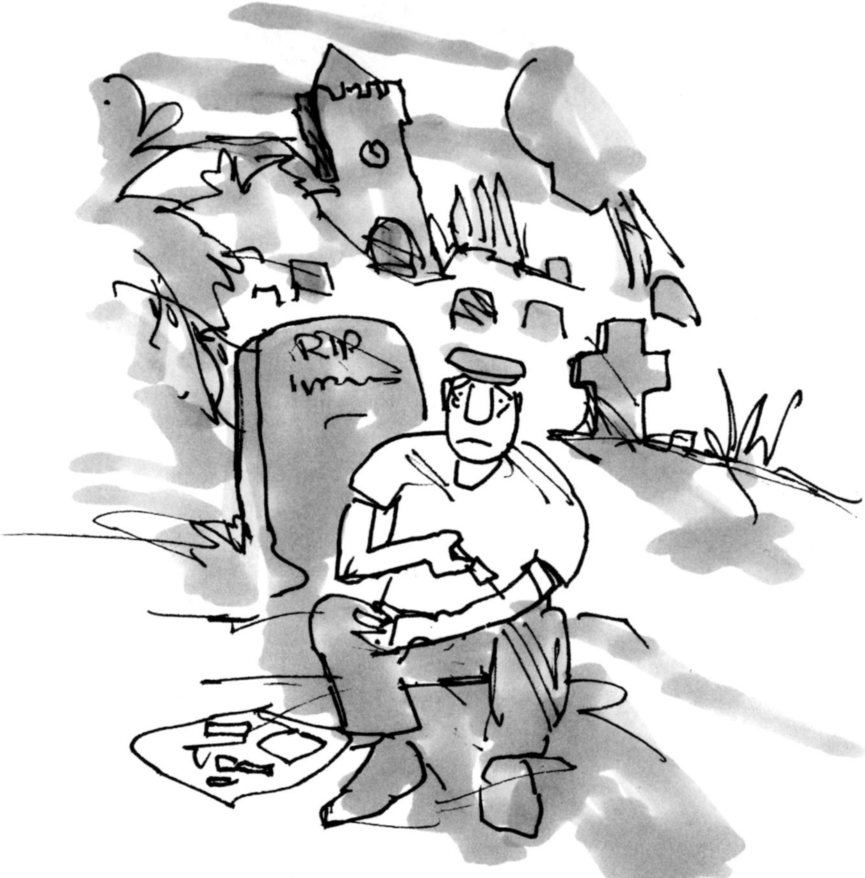
RIP

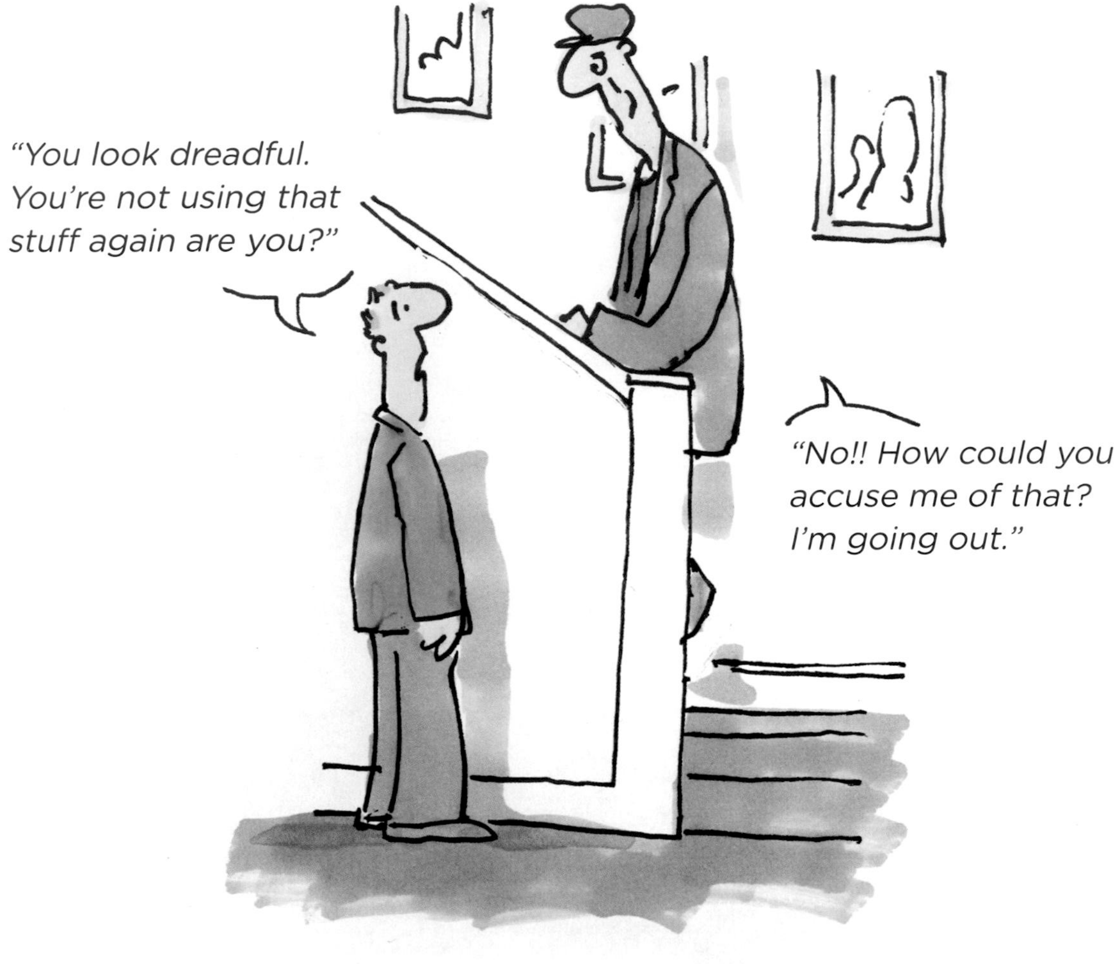
"You look dreadful. You're not using that stuff again are you?"
"No!! How could you accuse me of that? I'm going out."

"There's something wrong. Where is he?
I'm going to look for him."

"It's late and you've had a drink too.
He'll be OK."

"Paul, where are you? Oh, thank God, there you are!"

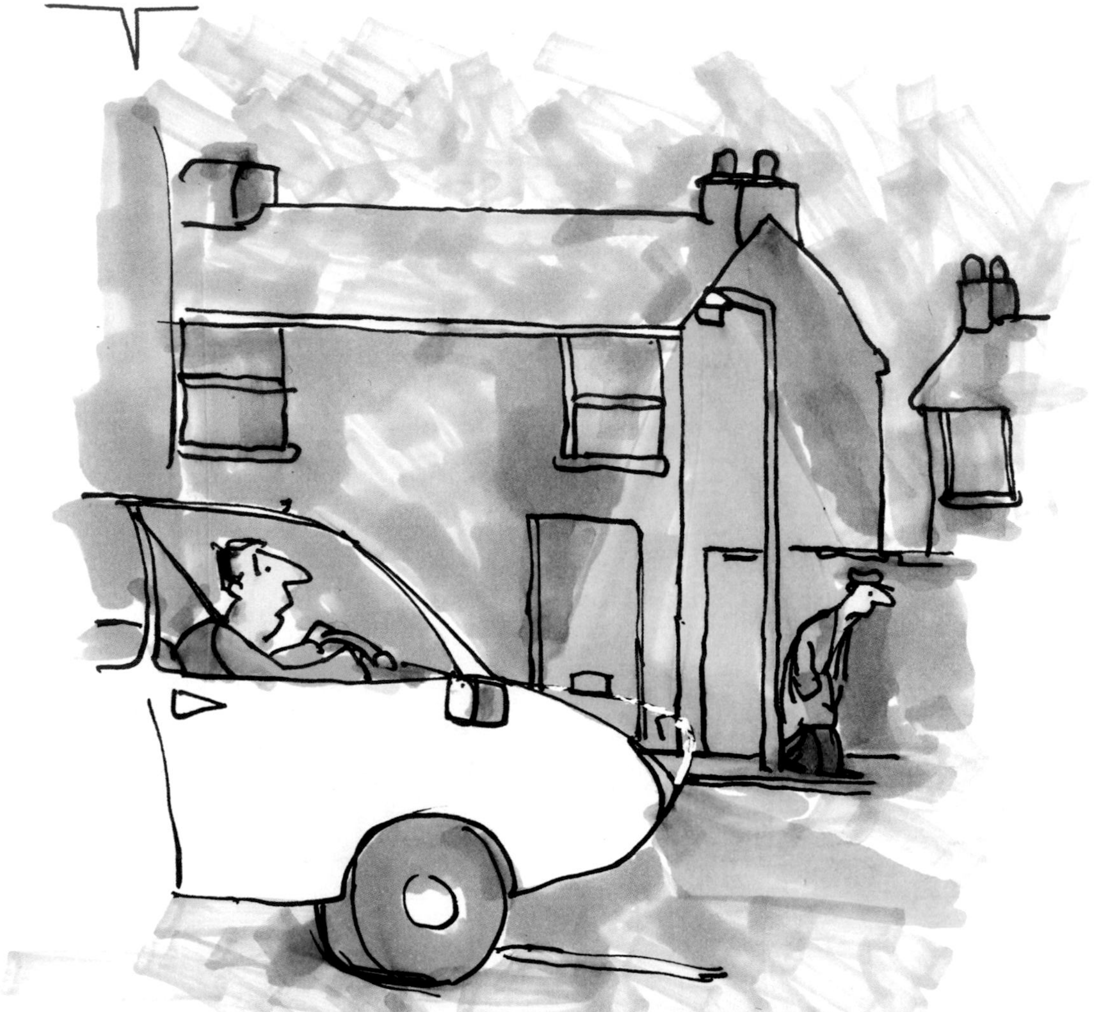

"Paul, what's wrong? What's going on?
You look awful... I'm scared."

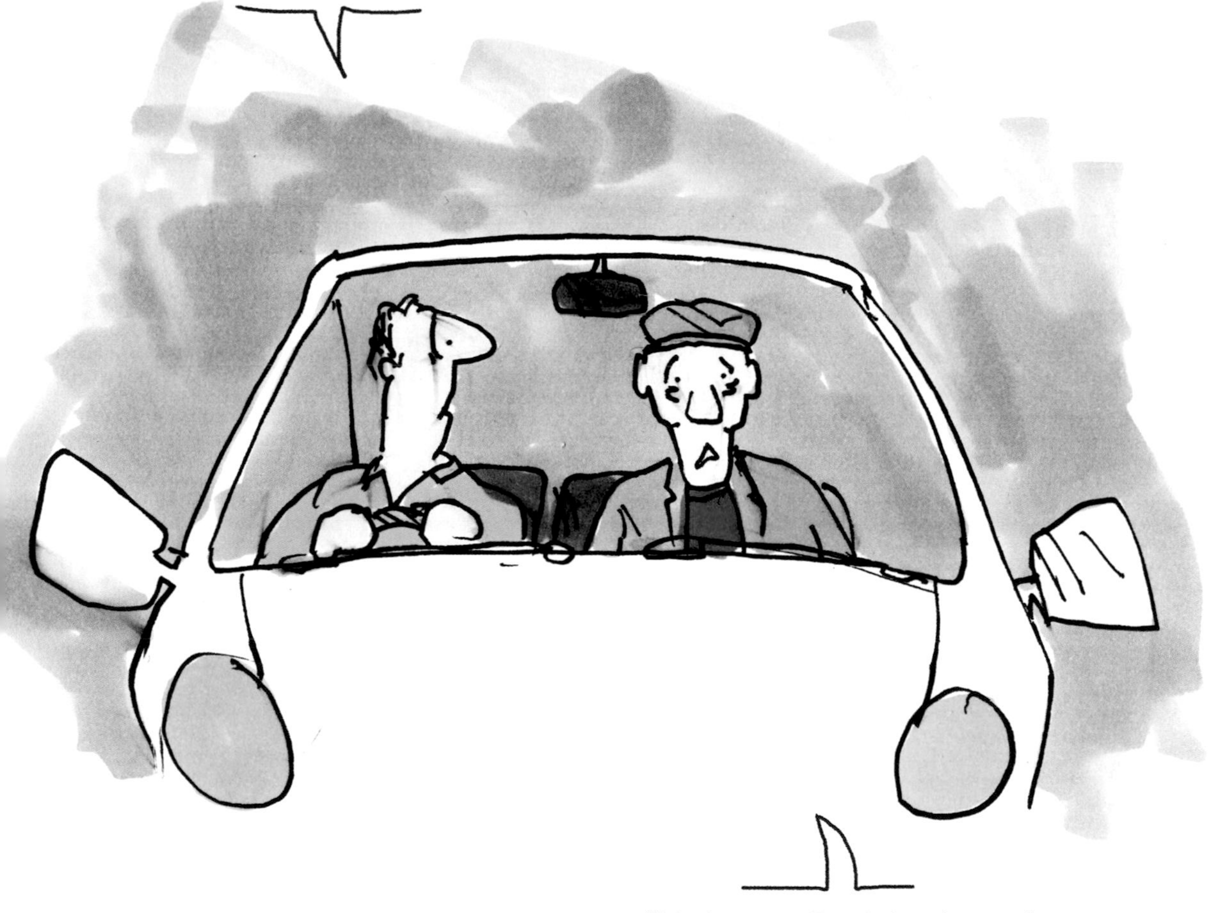

"Not now, Dad. Let's go home,
we'll talk in a bit."

"What's he doing? He said he'd be down to talk to us."

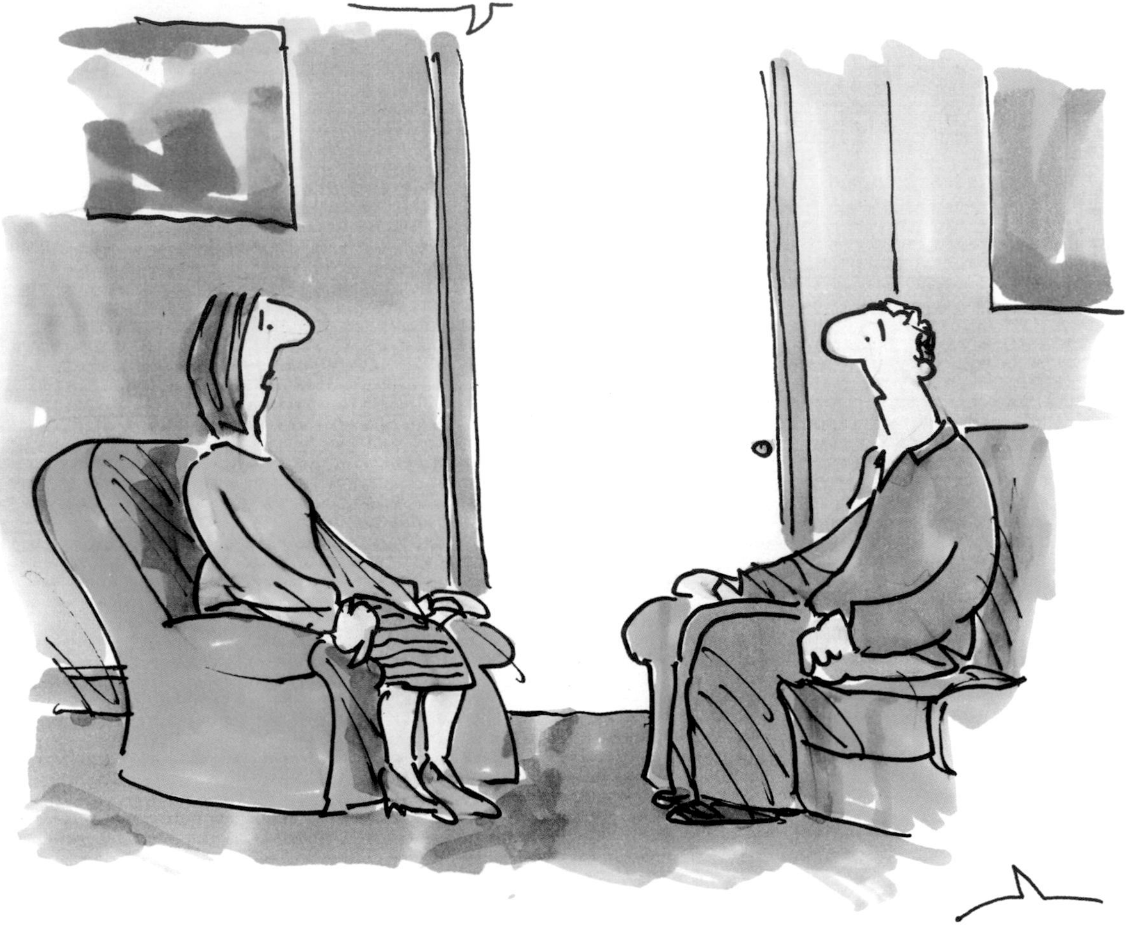

"I know, I know. I'll go and get him down. We need to talk."

"Shit, what are you doing? What's this?"

"Dad, it's not what you think… it's…"

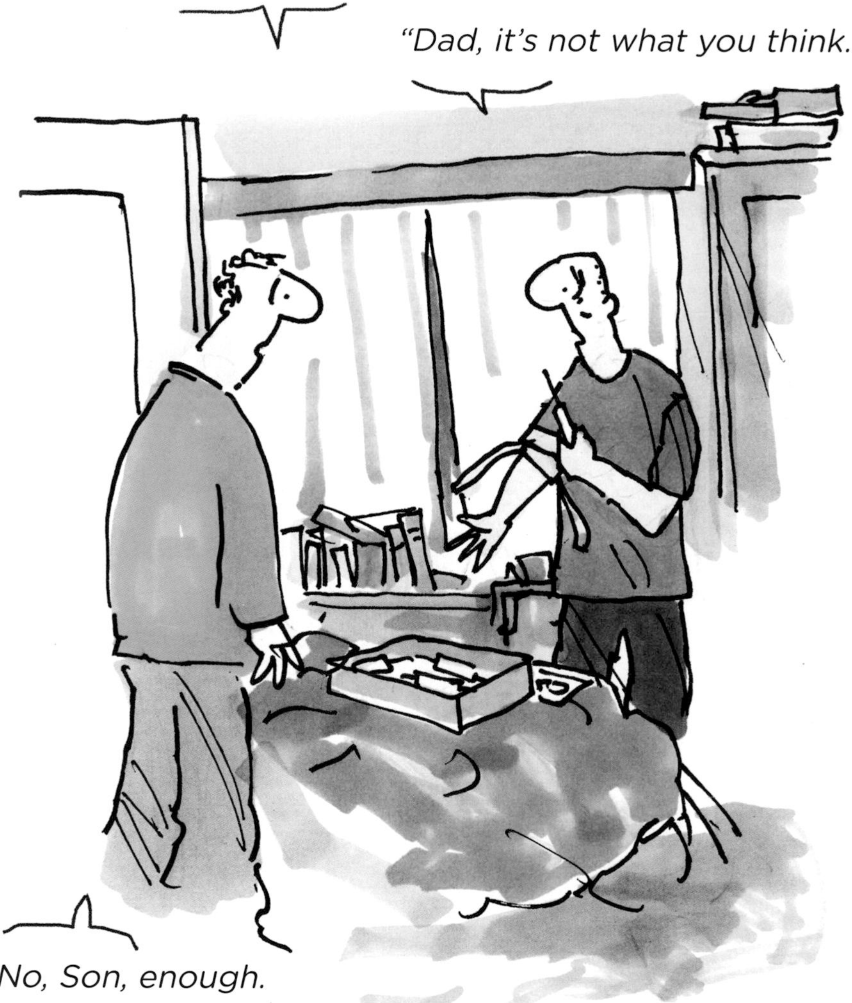

"No, Son, enough.
Let's stop this."

"I need help, Dad. Please help me."

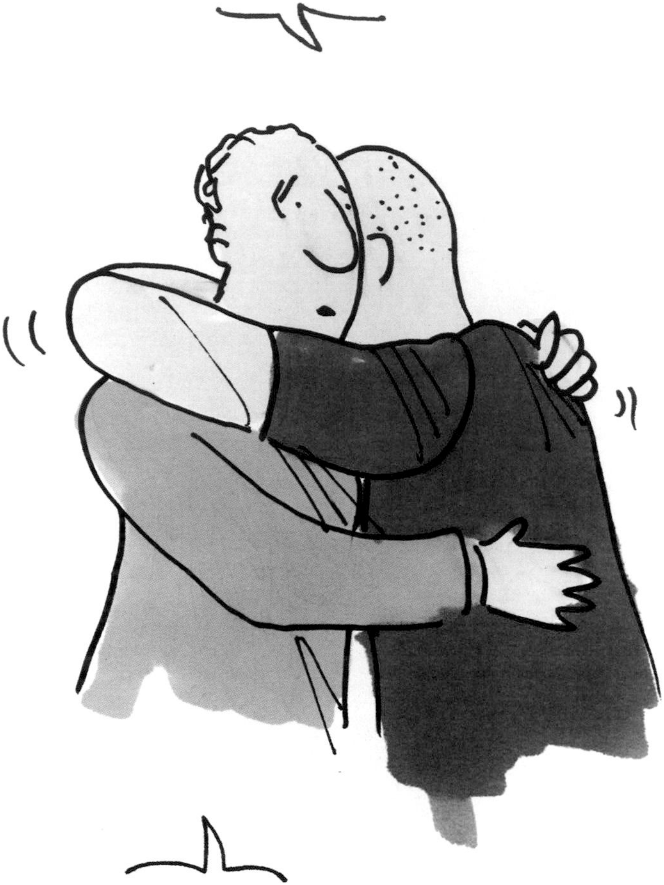

"We will... we'll fight this together."

We called in Bill – an intervention counsellor.
He recommended a private rehab centre in Bournemouth.
As far away from Hyde as possible.

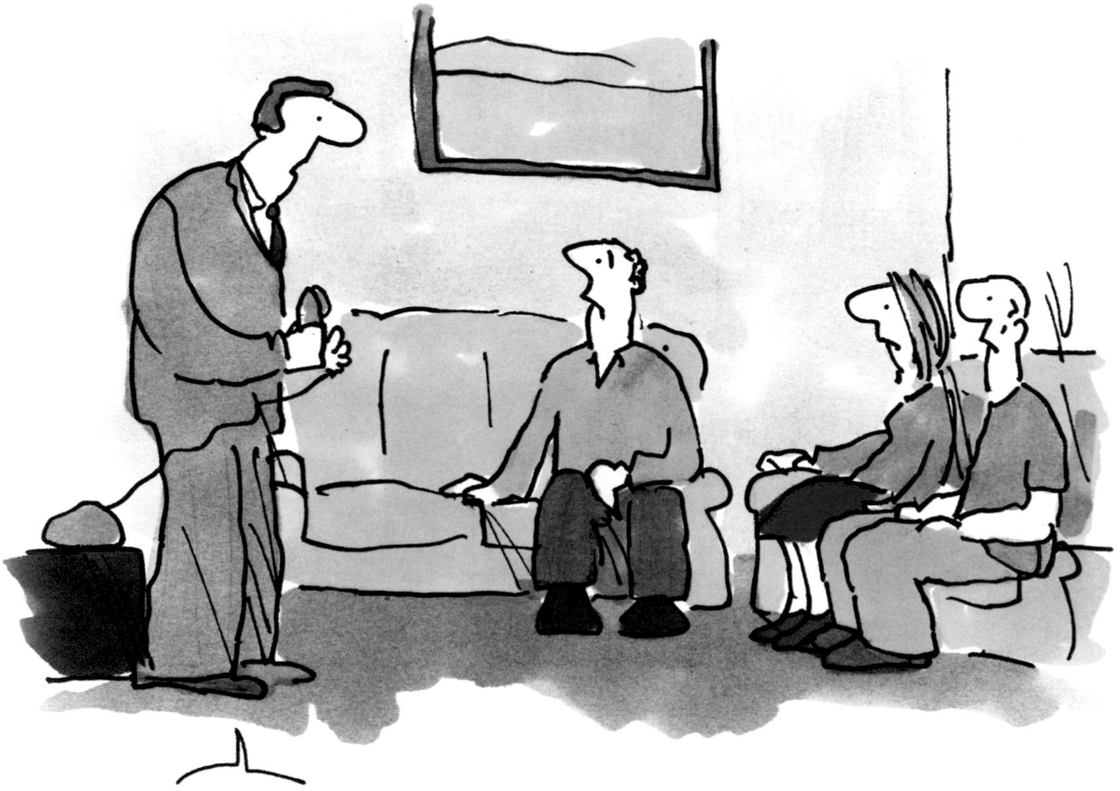

"You can be in there on Monday. I think you're ready and wanting this, Paul."

We dropped you in Bournemouth. The journey back was long and silent. We felt loss, hope, trepidation . . .

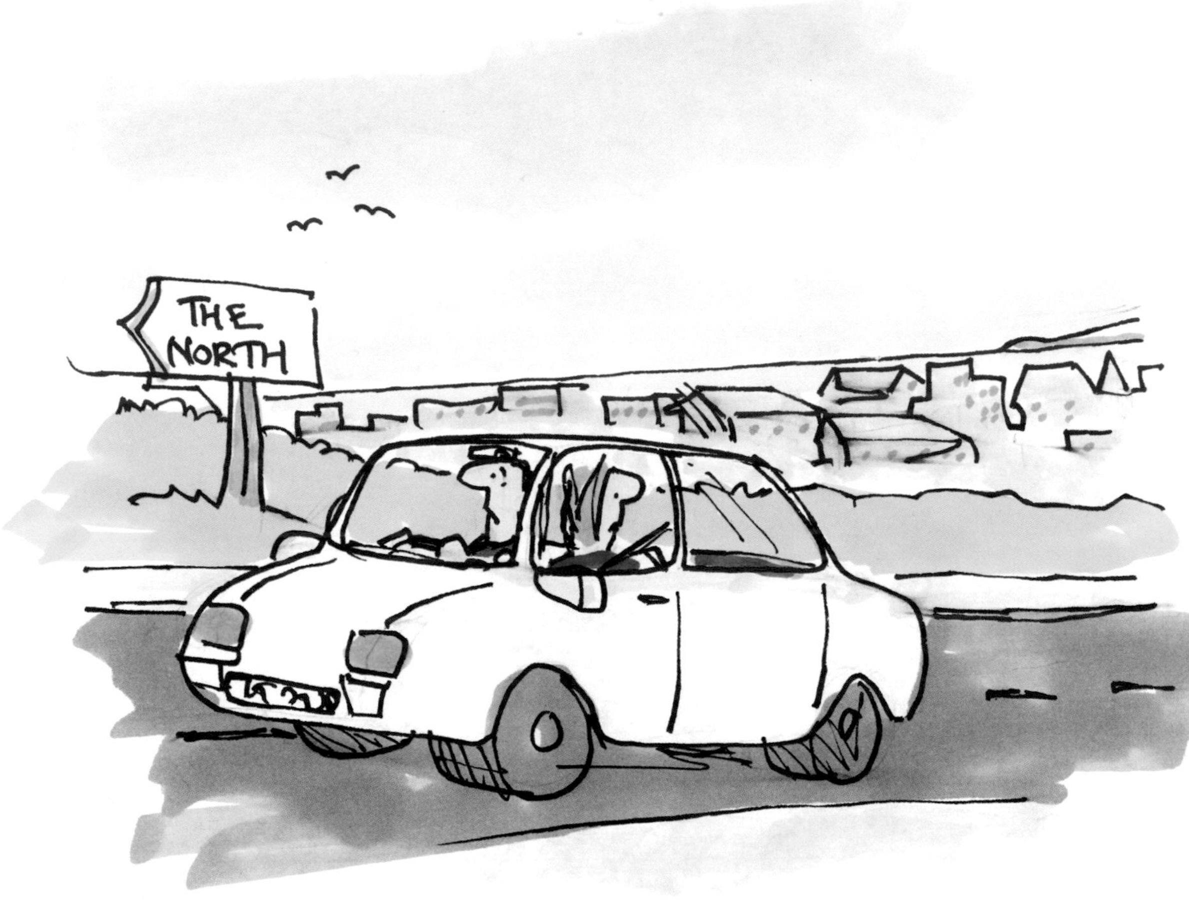
THE NORTH

I knew I was in danger. My body was torn with pain. I was ravaged – destroyed with fear and guilt. I was possessed by this demon and I needed help.

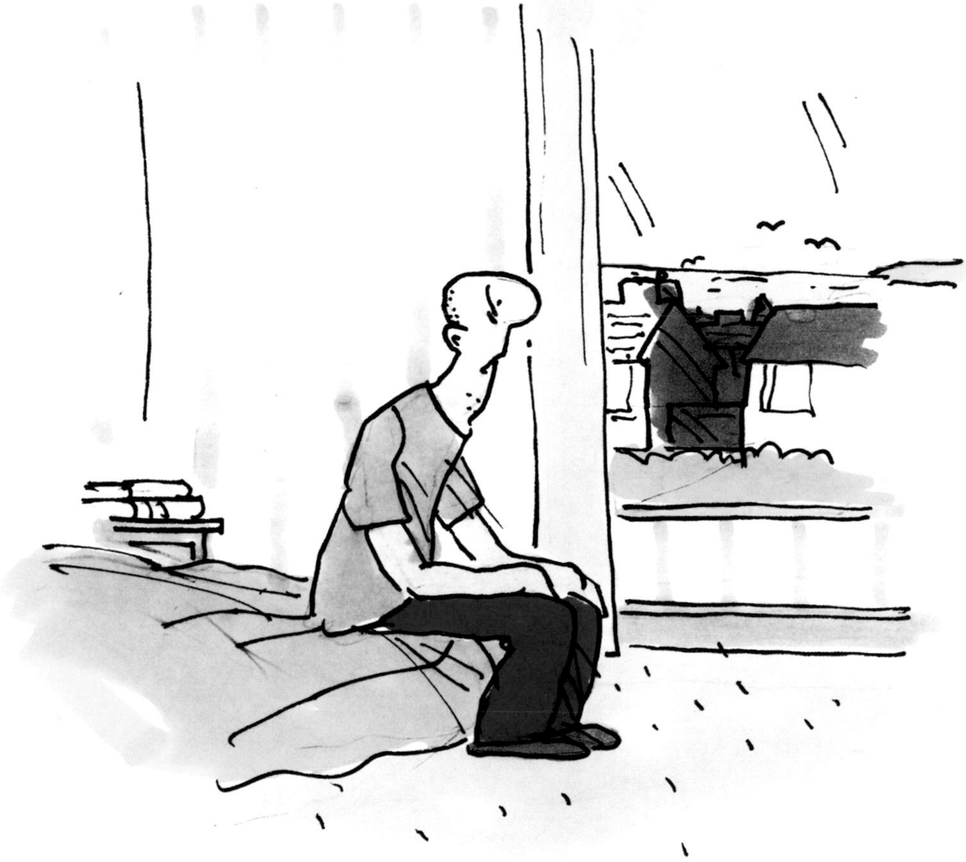

Detox was so hard. I didn't sleep for days. Every muscle, every joint screamed in pain.

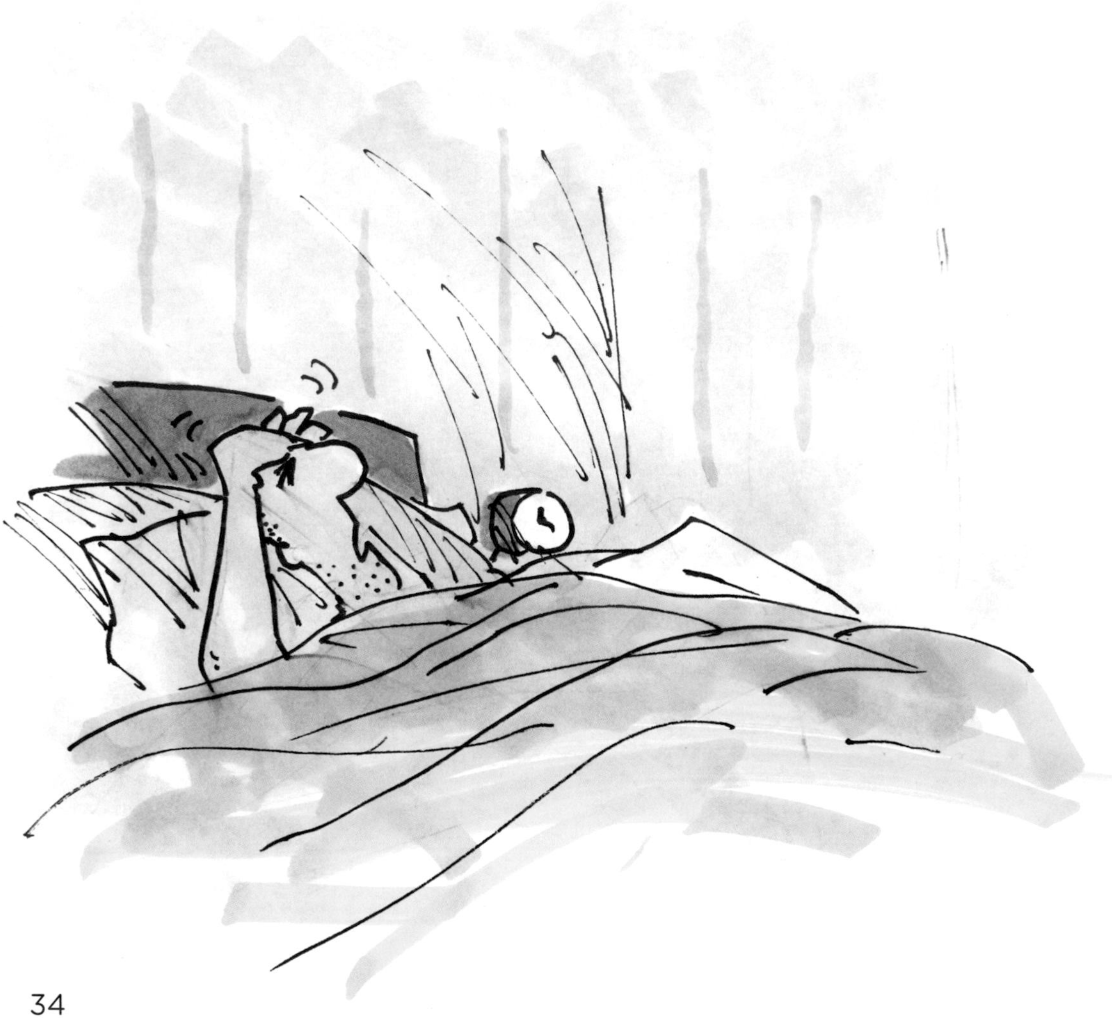

I settled in slowly at the centre. The people were friendly and welcoming but I was cautious. As I rebuilt my strength and confidence, I began to connect.

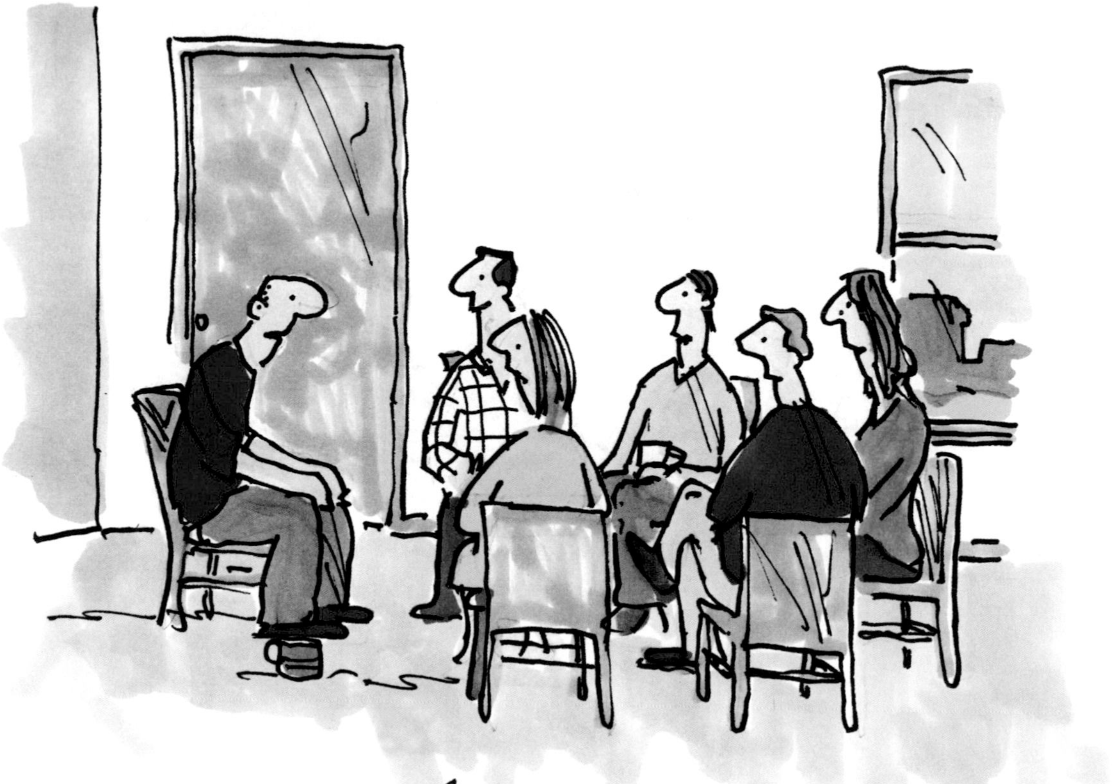

"Good point, Paul."

"Ha, yes. I know that feeling."

I began to find my feet. I had new friends. We bonded and trusted each other.

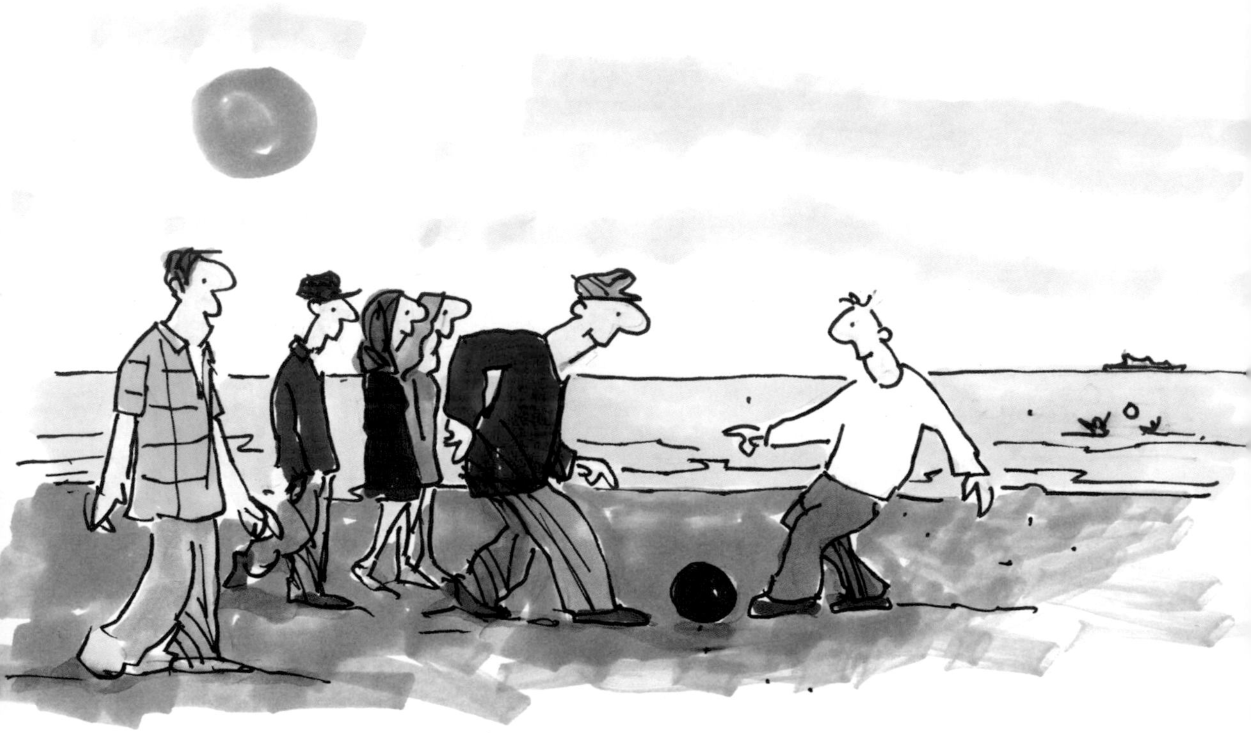

Your nine-month stay in rehab was coming to an end.

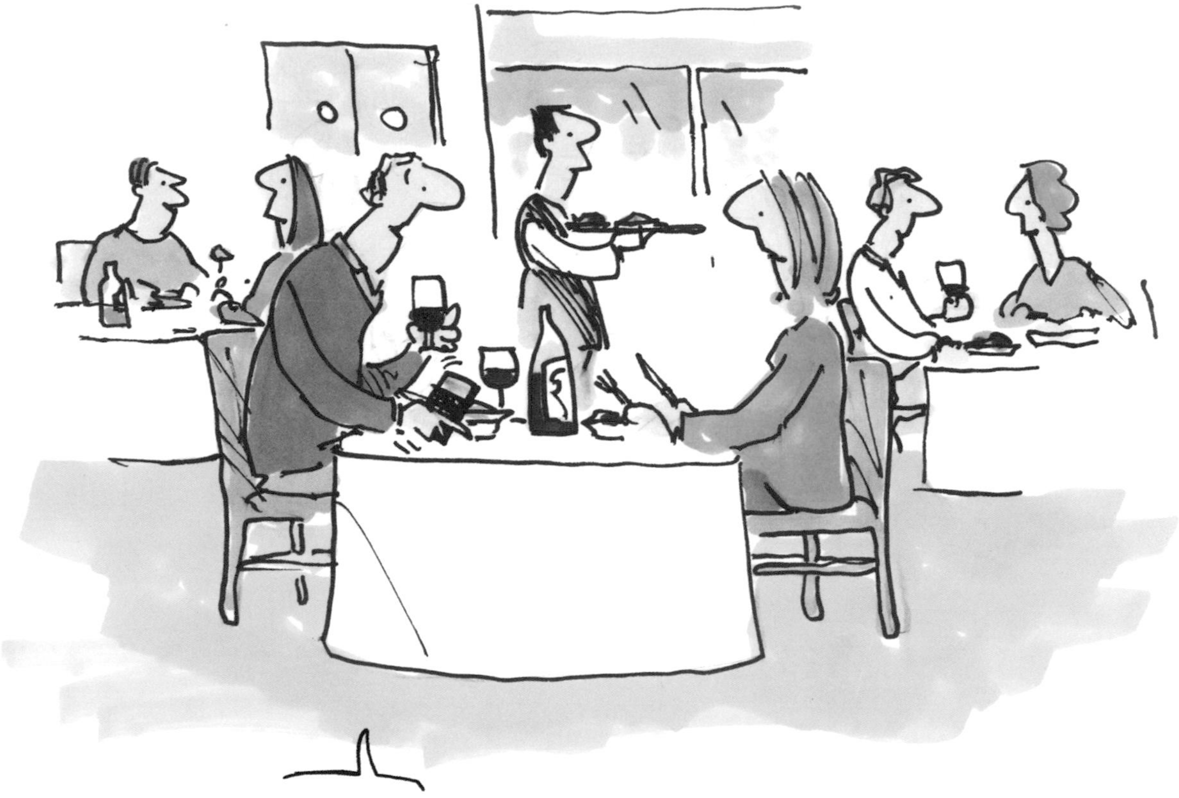

"That was Paul on the phone. He wants to stay in Bournemouth. He wants us to help him find a flat."

But I soon found that the demons hadn't been banished...
I started drinking more or less straight away.

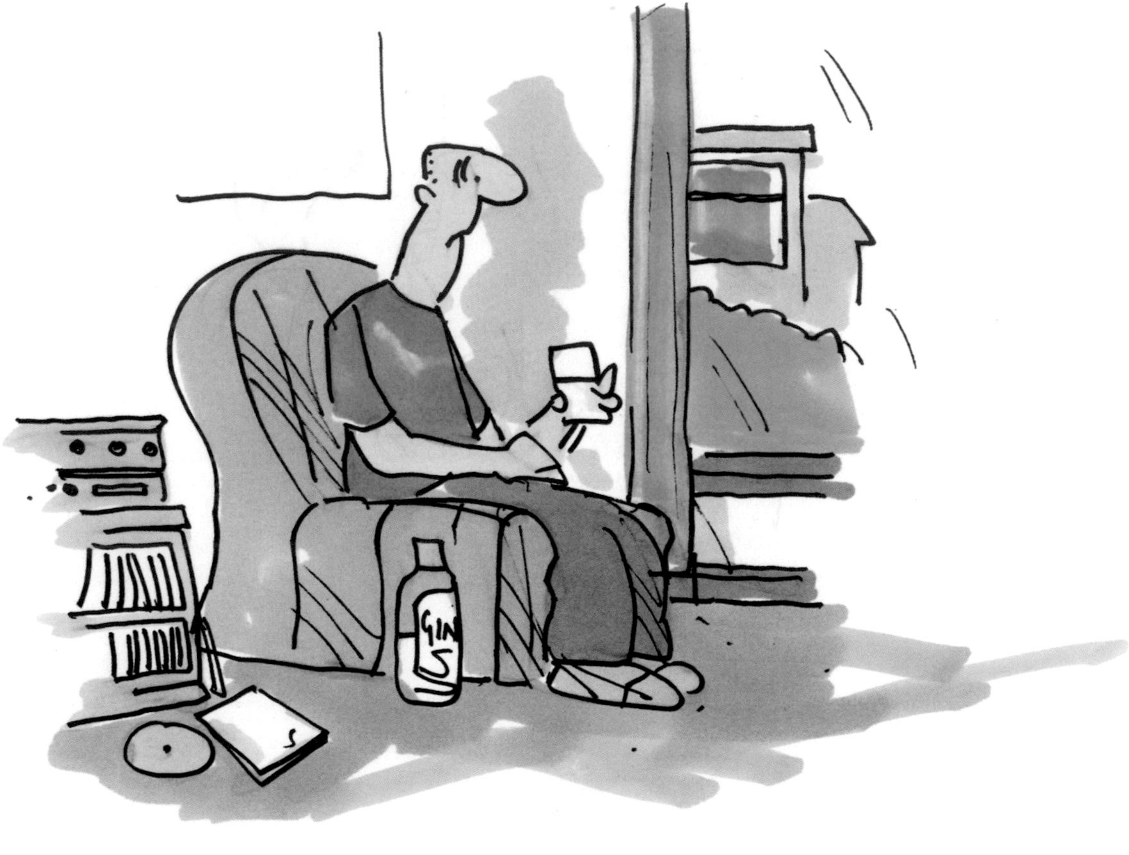
GIN

Before long I was back on the street scoring, selling what I had, borrowing... I was still in the grip of my addiction.

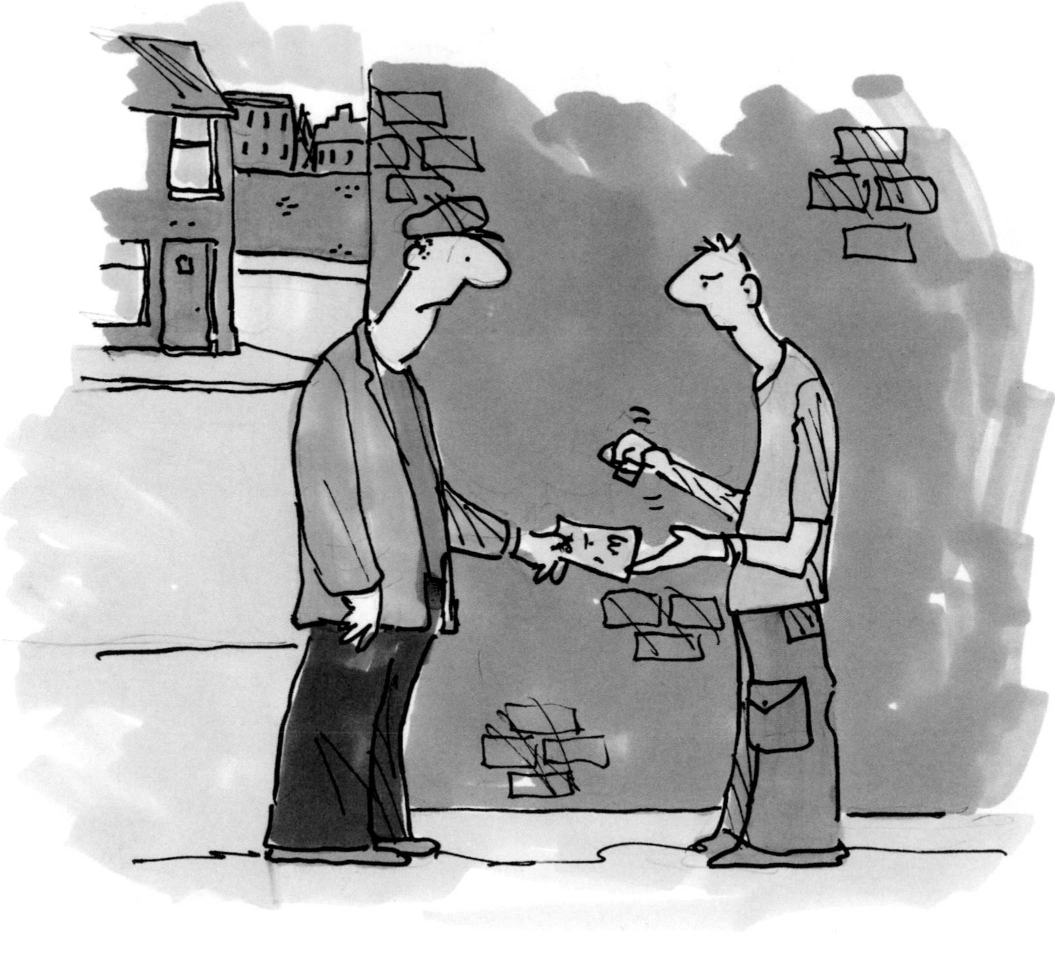

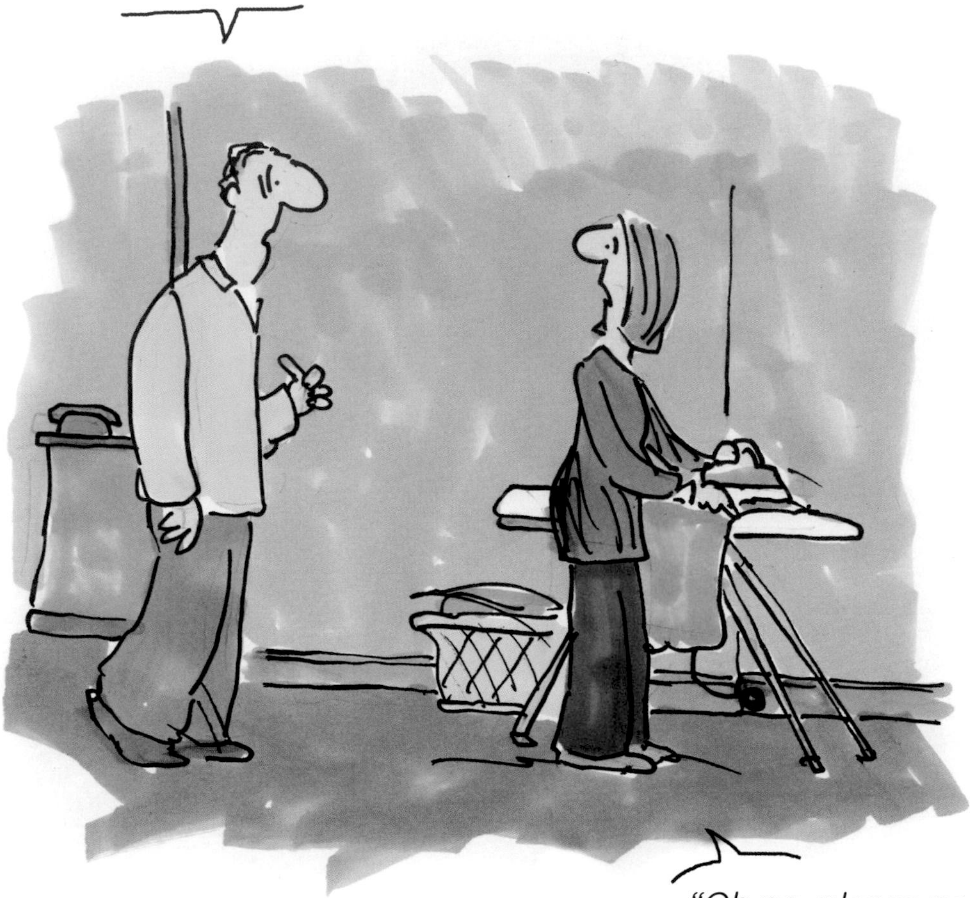
"That was Paul's landlord. He's accusing him of using drugs in the flat. That's why he's borrowing money again. He must be using."
"Oh no, please no..."

My flat was empty. I'd sold everything... again! But things were going to get worse...

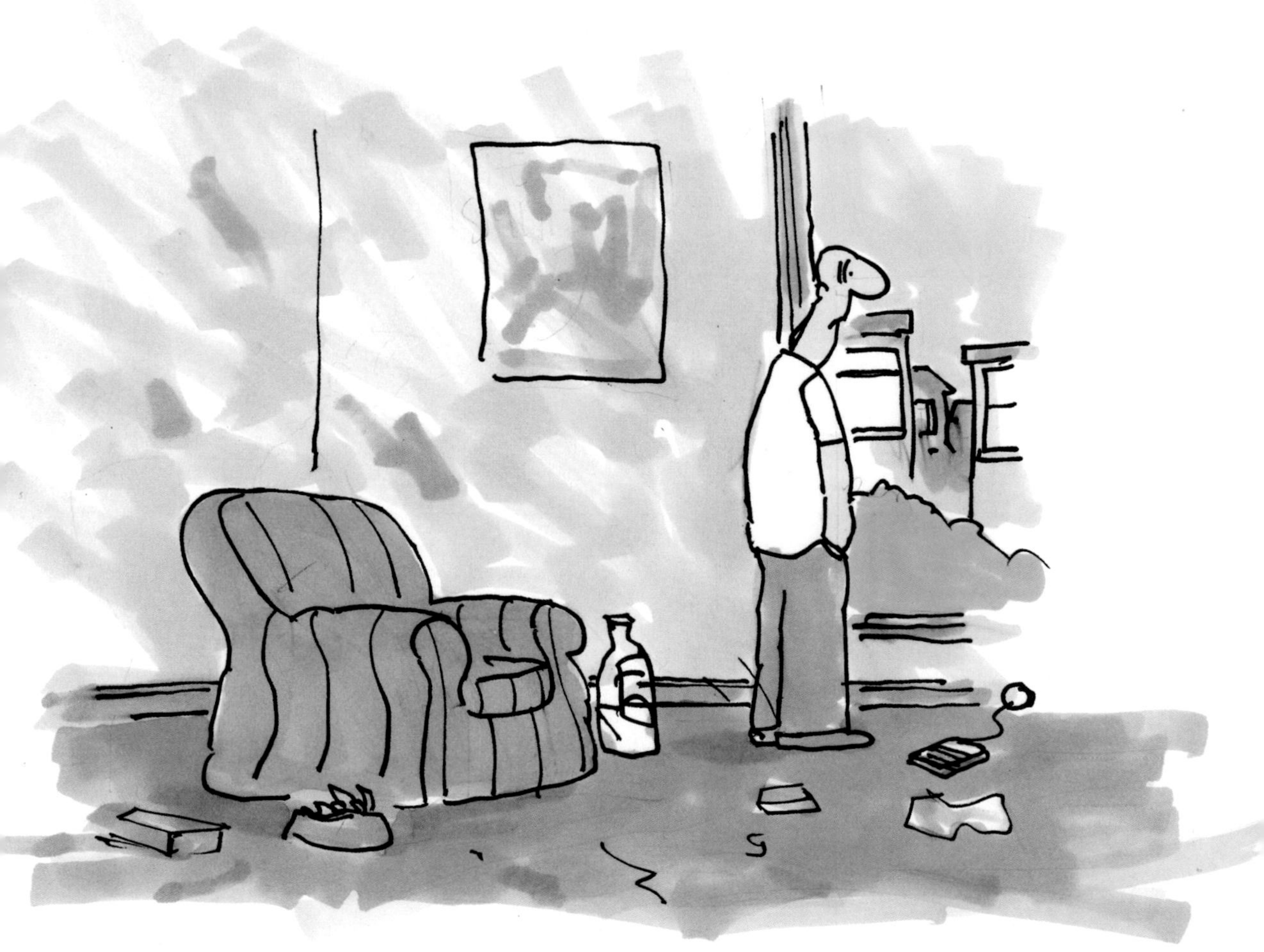

I was rushed to the hospital,
my body not used to the drug.

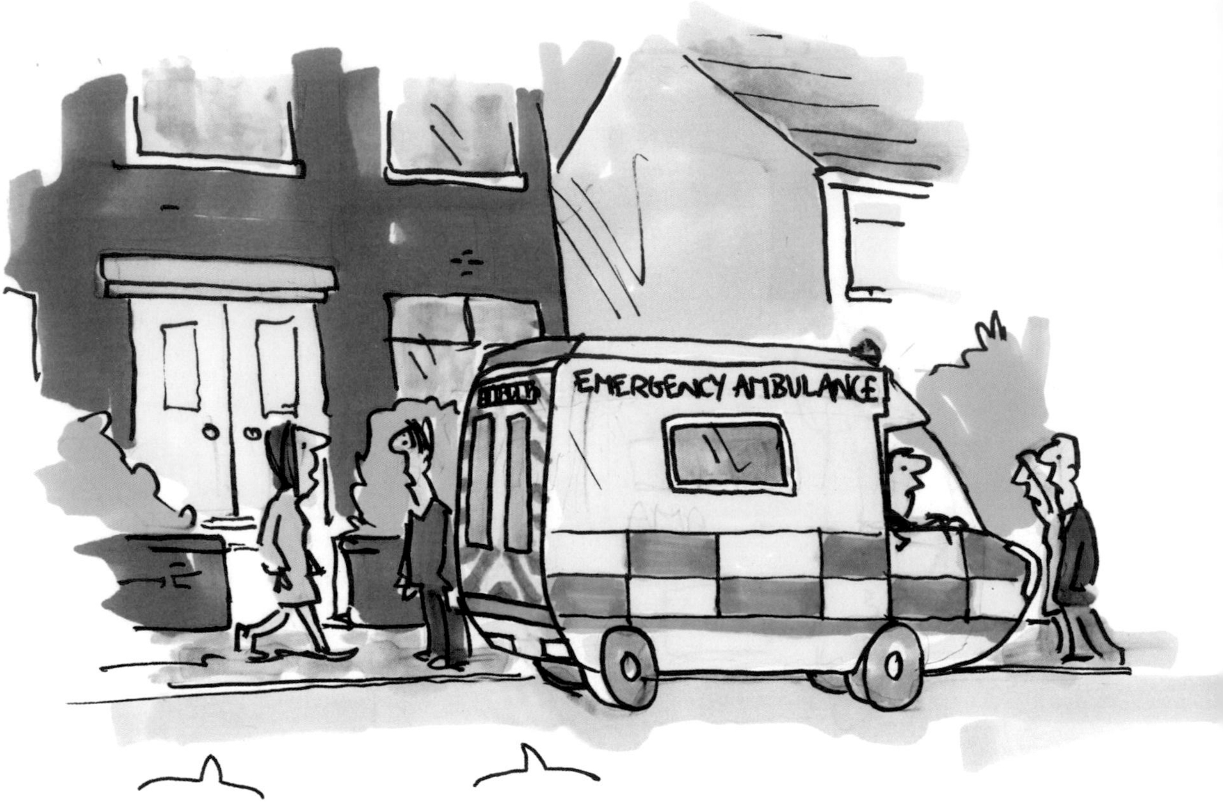
EMERGENCY AMBULANCE

"What's happened?" *"It's Paul, he's OD'd!"*

The news shattered us. The light went out at the end of the tunnel. I had no idea what to do next. Then at a party I met wonderful Tom.

"What do you do, Tom?"

"I'm Head of Drug and Alcohol Recovery in Lancashire."

I could have sat anywhere at that party... it was fate. Tom introduced me to Peter and the wonderful world of LUF (Lancashire User Forum).

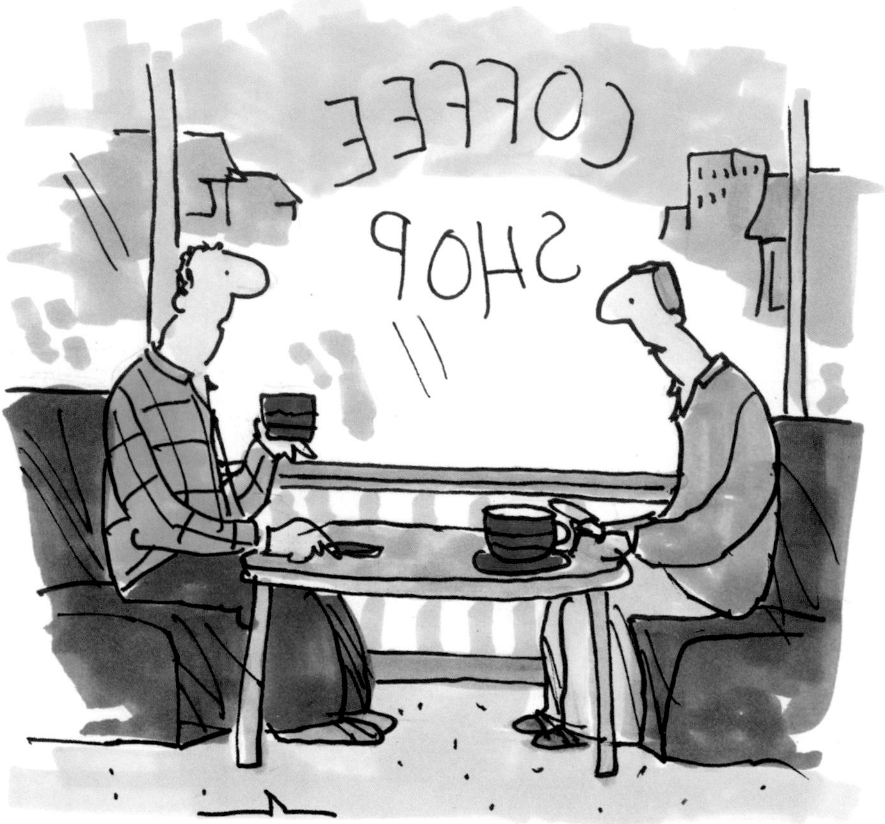
COFFEE
SHOP

"What should I do, Peter?"

"Get him out of Bournemouth. Parachute him into our world. Let us take care of him."

I left Bournemouth with a heavy heart and many regrets. I felt I had failed and let people down. I was lucky to be alive but I was running out of luck and I knew this.

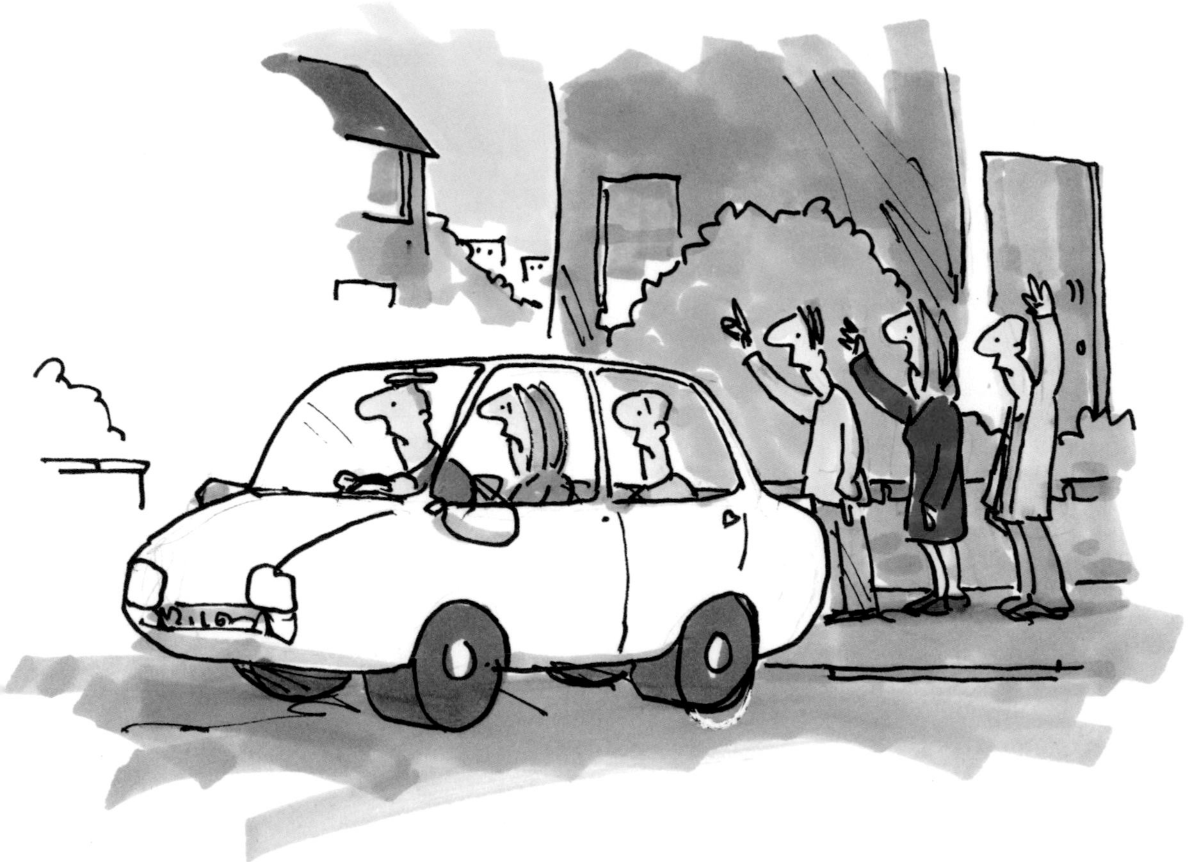

The LUF group were amazing. I felt I was part of a movement. No one judged me because they were all in the same boat. I felt worthwhile again. Their love and energy was infectious.

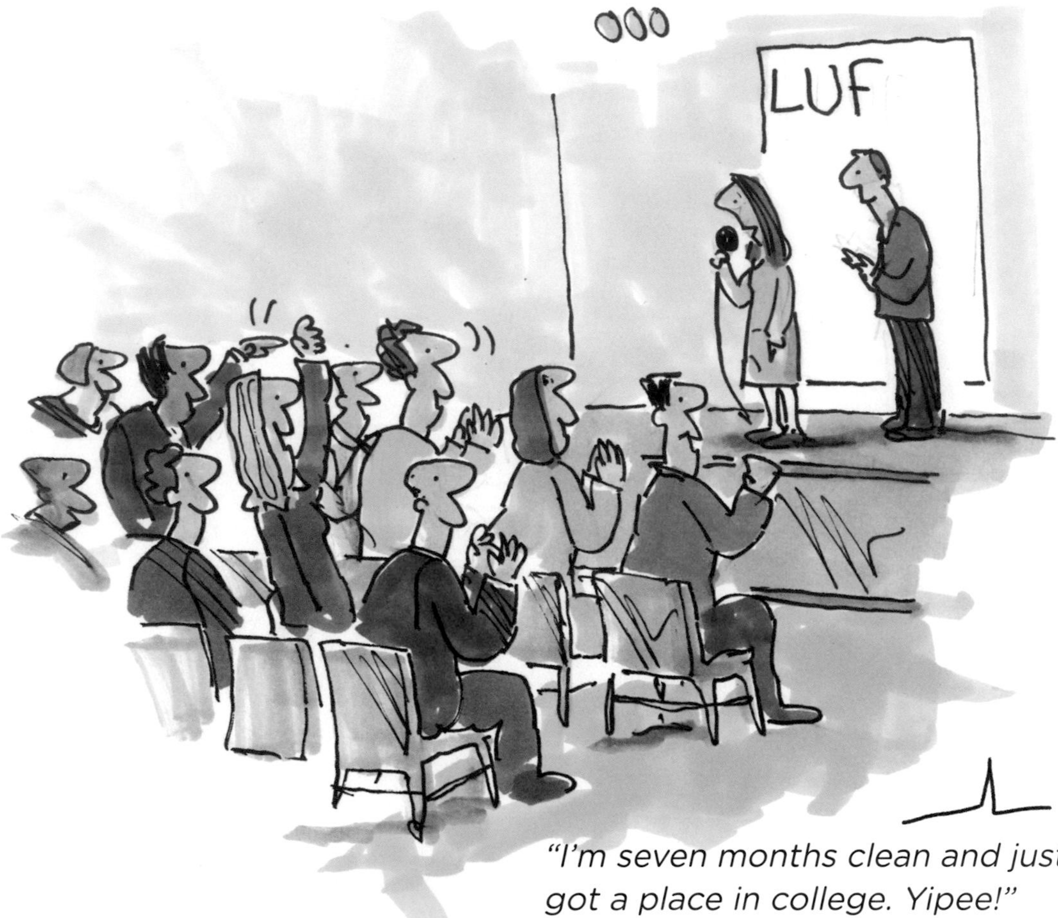
LUF

"I'm seven months clean and just got a place in college. Yipee!"

We were a family. We wanted to show we were a valuable part of the community, not pariahs.

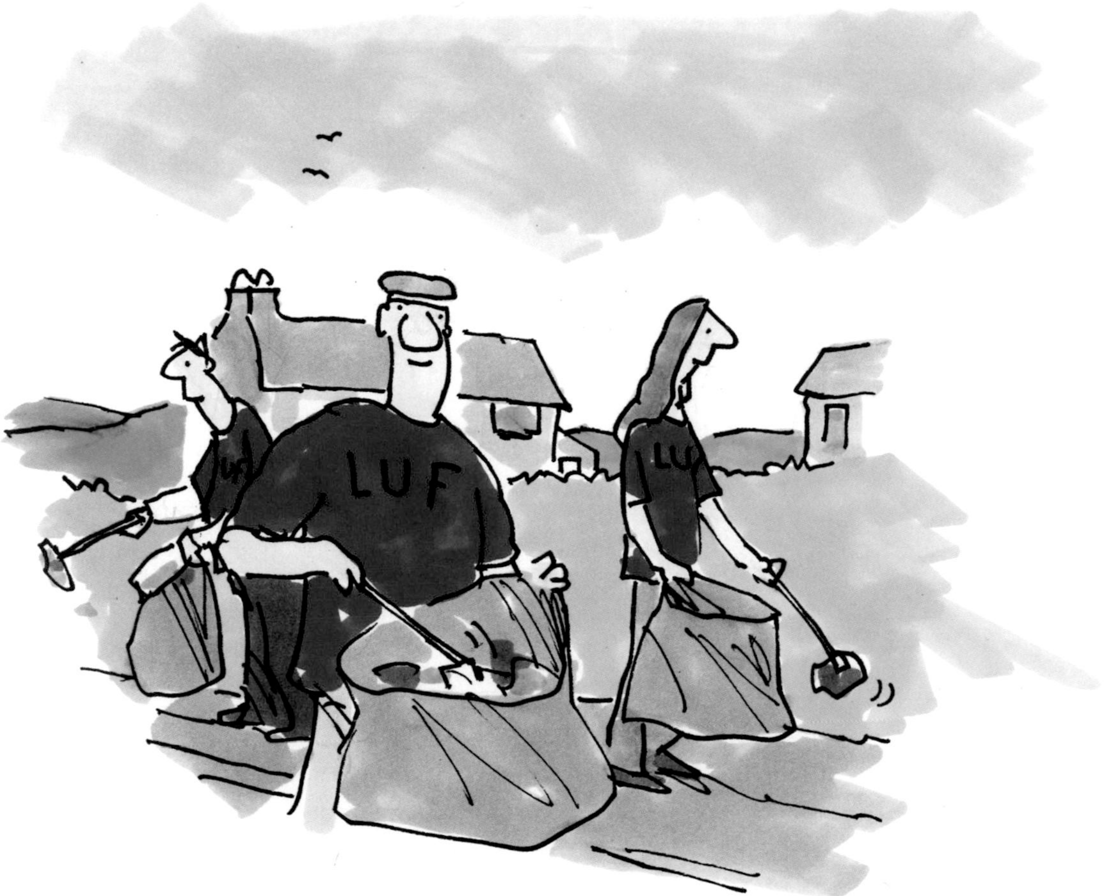
LUF

I was on the fabulous LUF barge one day with Peter when Dave the LUF video-maker introduced me to photography. I was smitten.

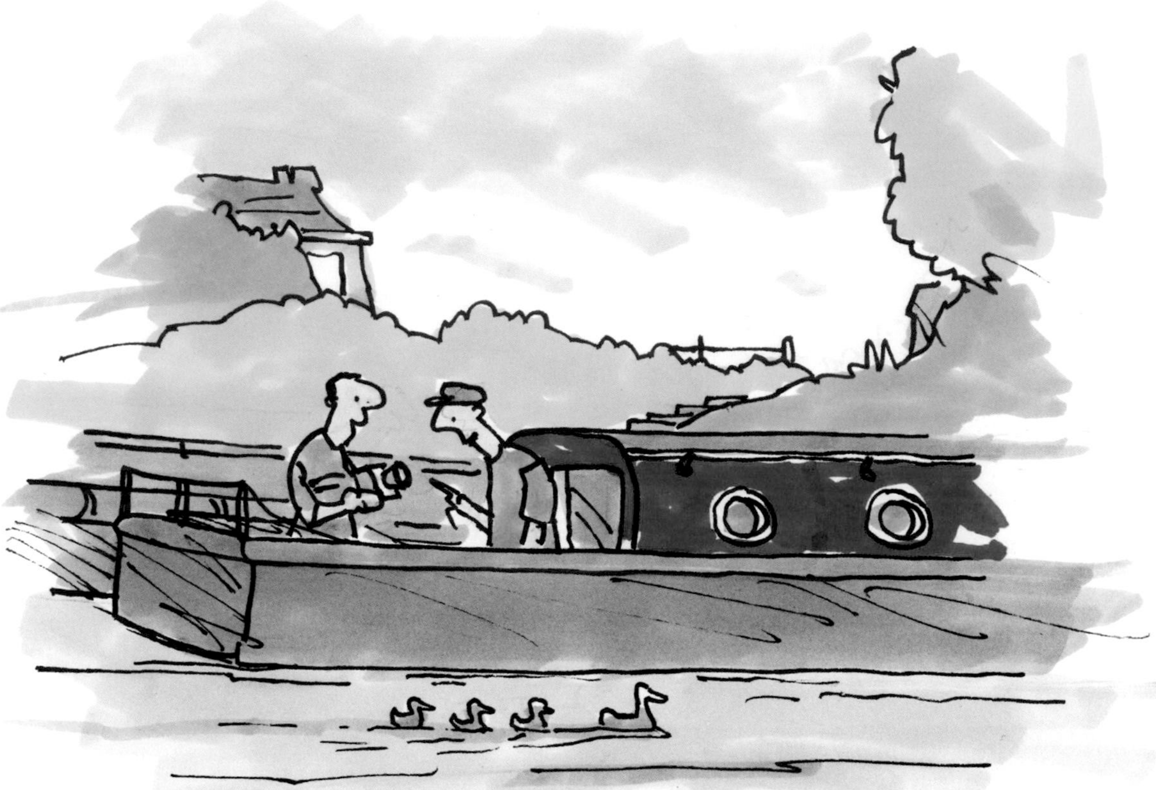

My life began to have meaning. I began to look forward to things. I had ambitions, goals...

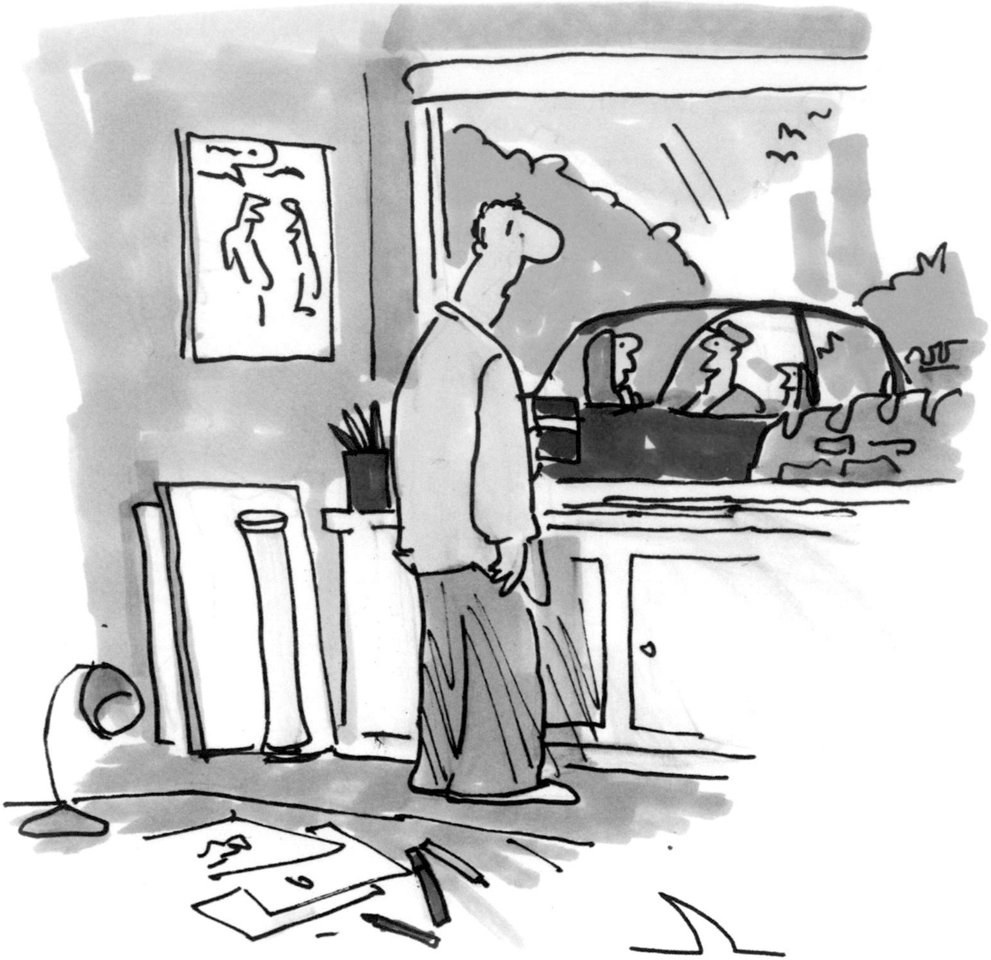

"Hello... who's this dropping Paul off?"

At my primary school reunion, after all those years,
I met my school crush Sarah. We started seeing each other.

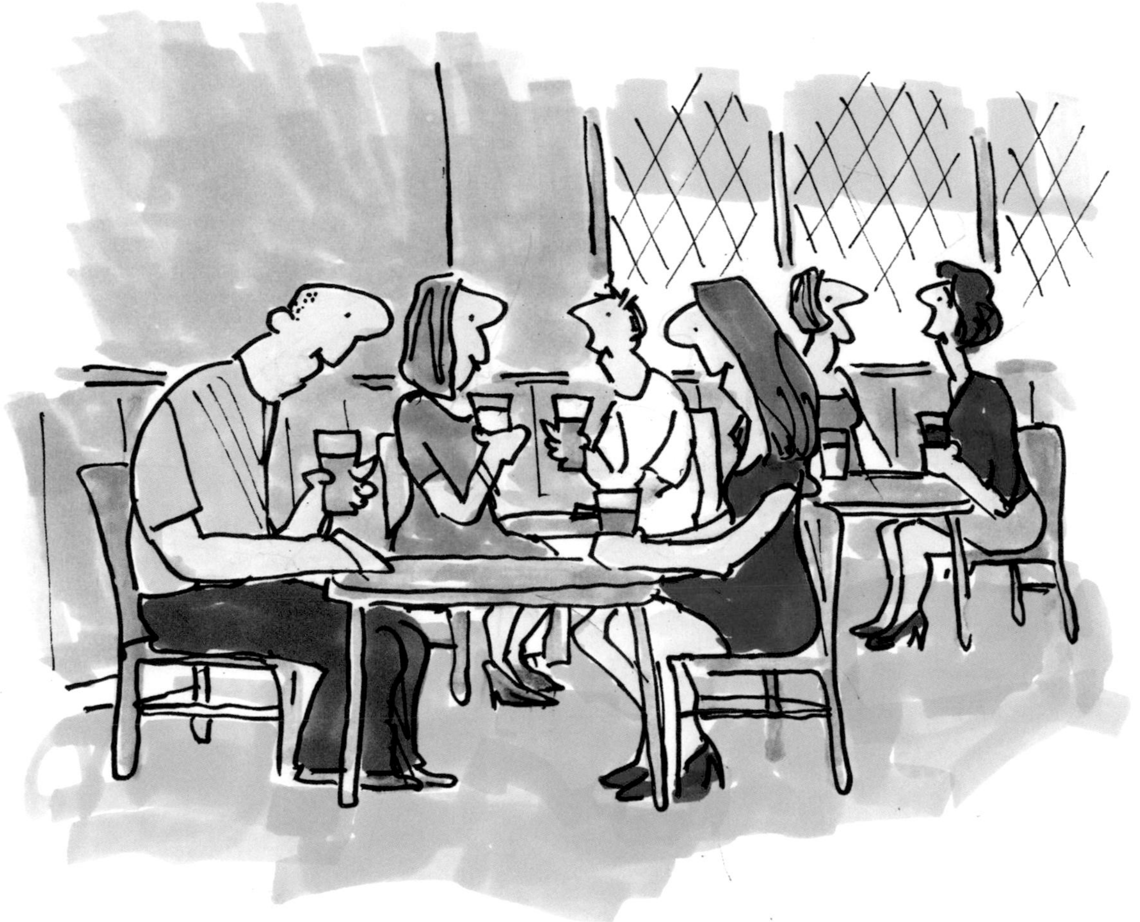

The moment you introduced us to Sarah and Pheobe, we got on. We became friends. They were special.

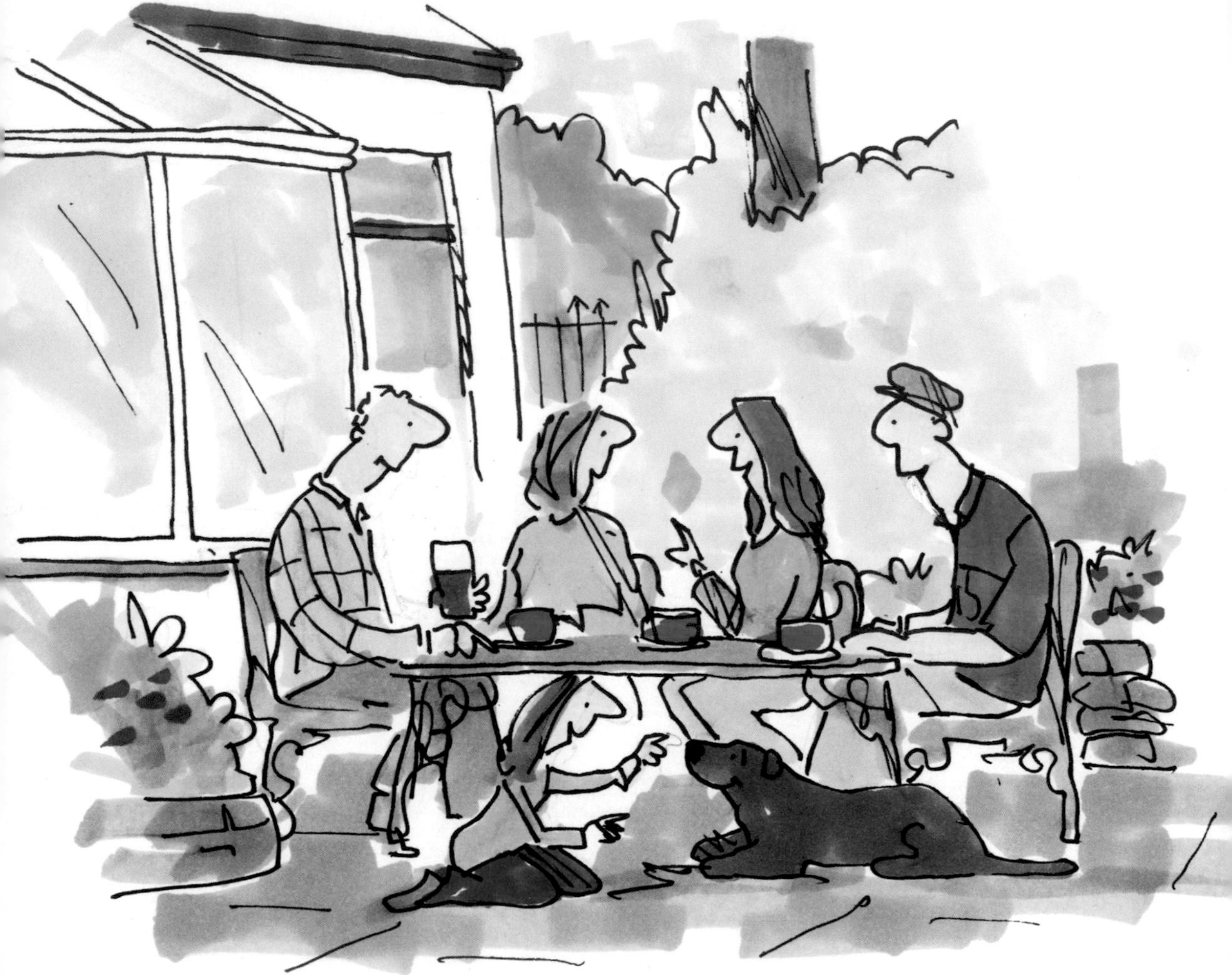

As my relationship with Sarah and Pheobe grew, so did my love and understanding of photography.

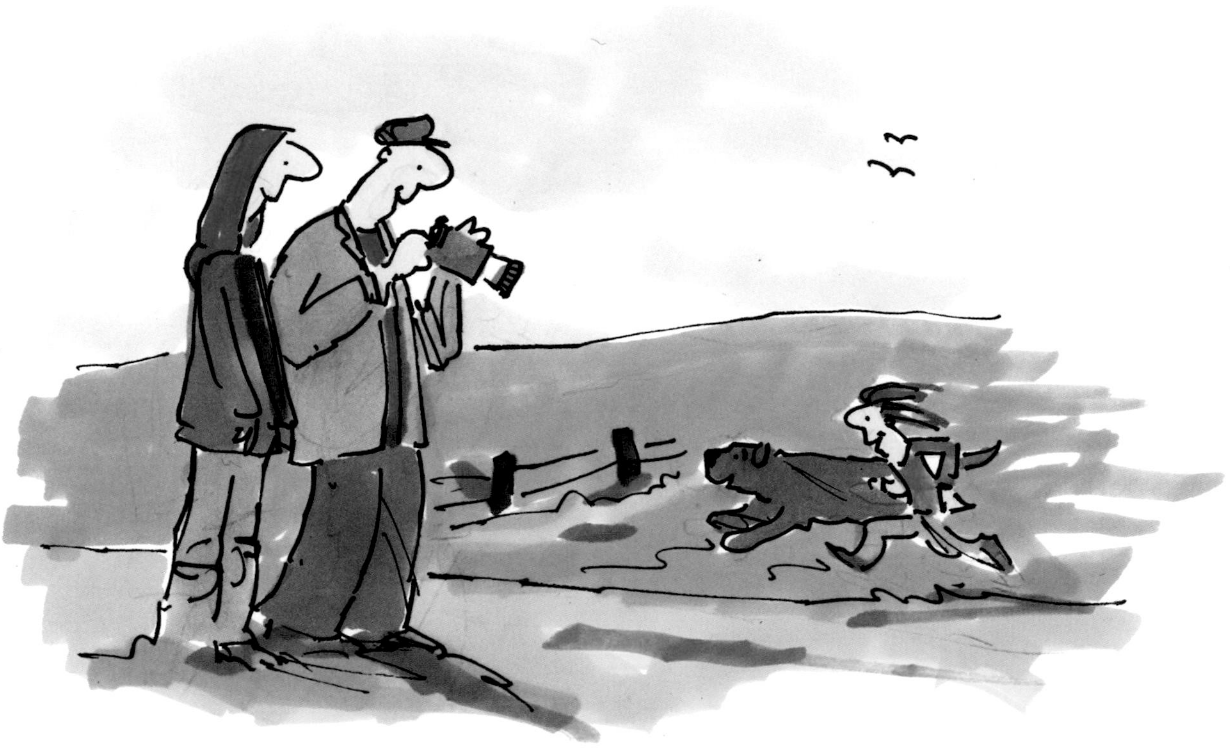

Yes, we realised you had a very special talent.

I was getting commissions – weddings, events, even a full page in an international rock magazine.

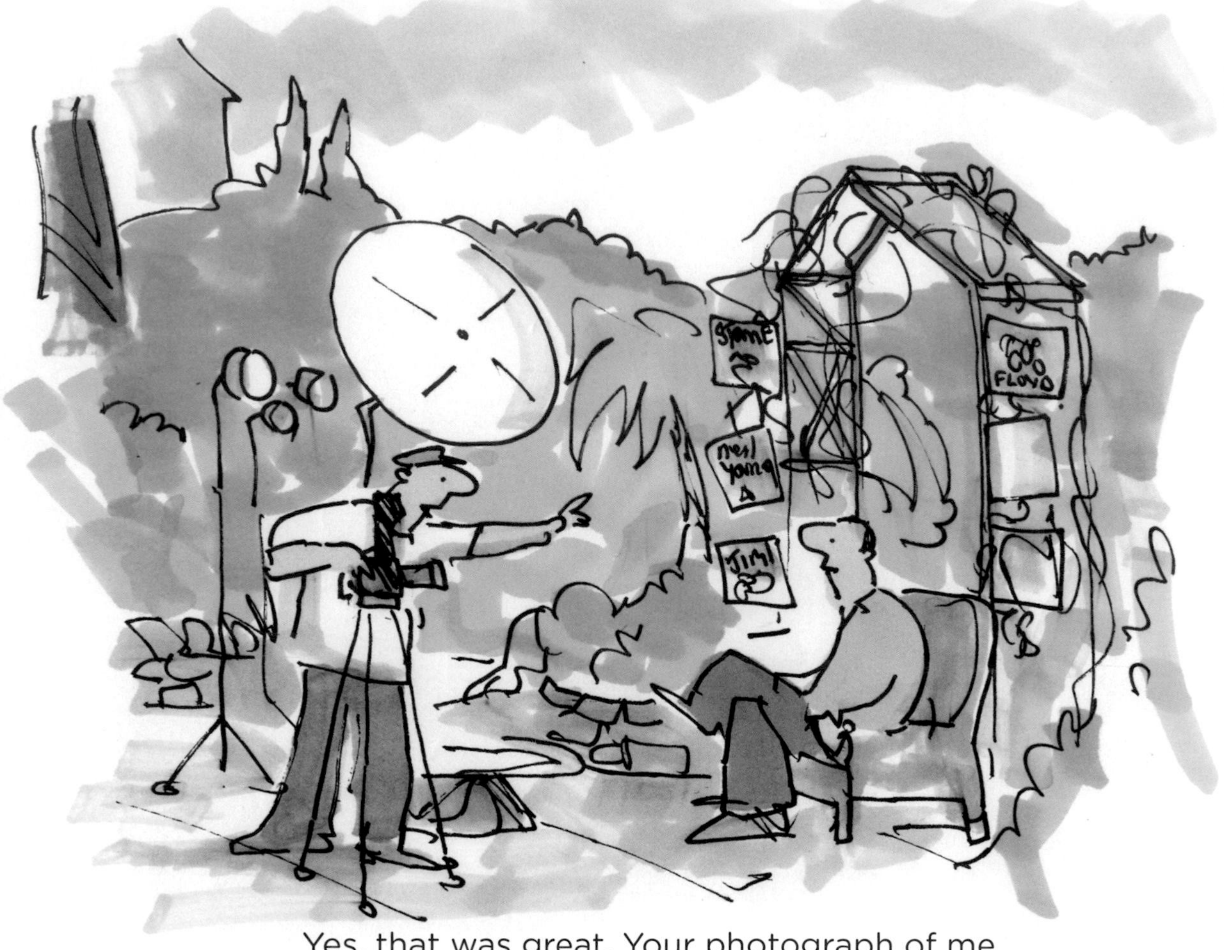
neil young
Jimi
FLOYD

Yes, that was great. Your photograph of me to go with my interview.

As for me, my mind was free. Ideas poured out of me.
I felt reborn. A huge weight had been lifted.

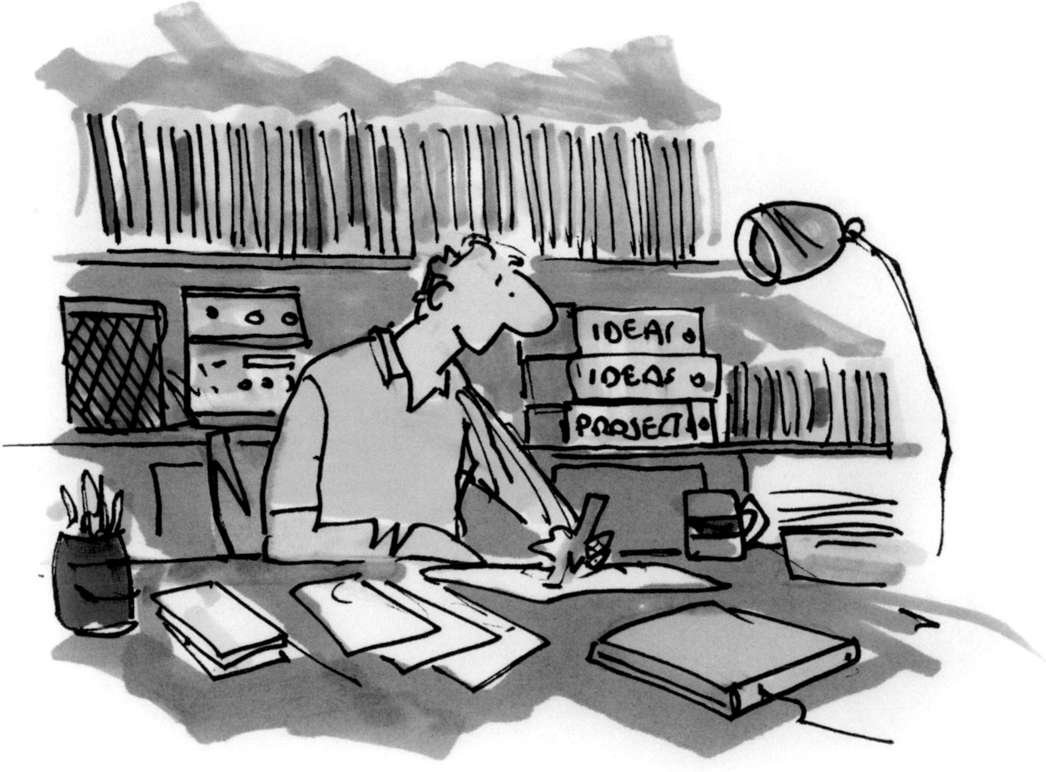
IDEAS
IDEAS
PROJECT

Then at a New Year's Eve party, Pheobe made an announcement.

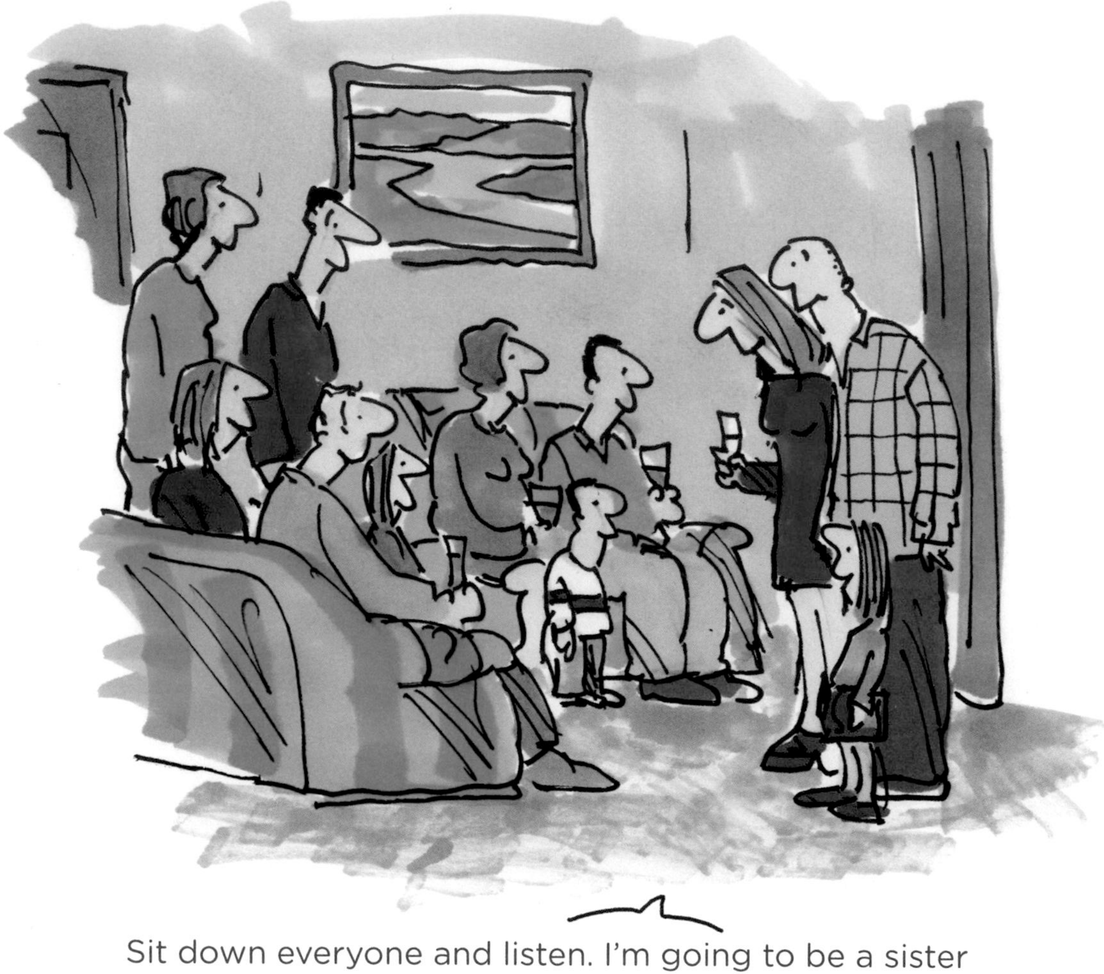

Sit down everyone and listen. I'm going to be a sister because mummy's having a baby!

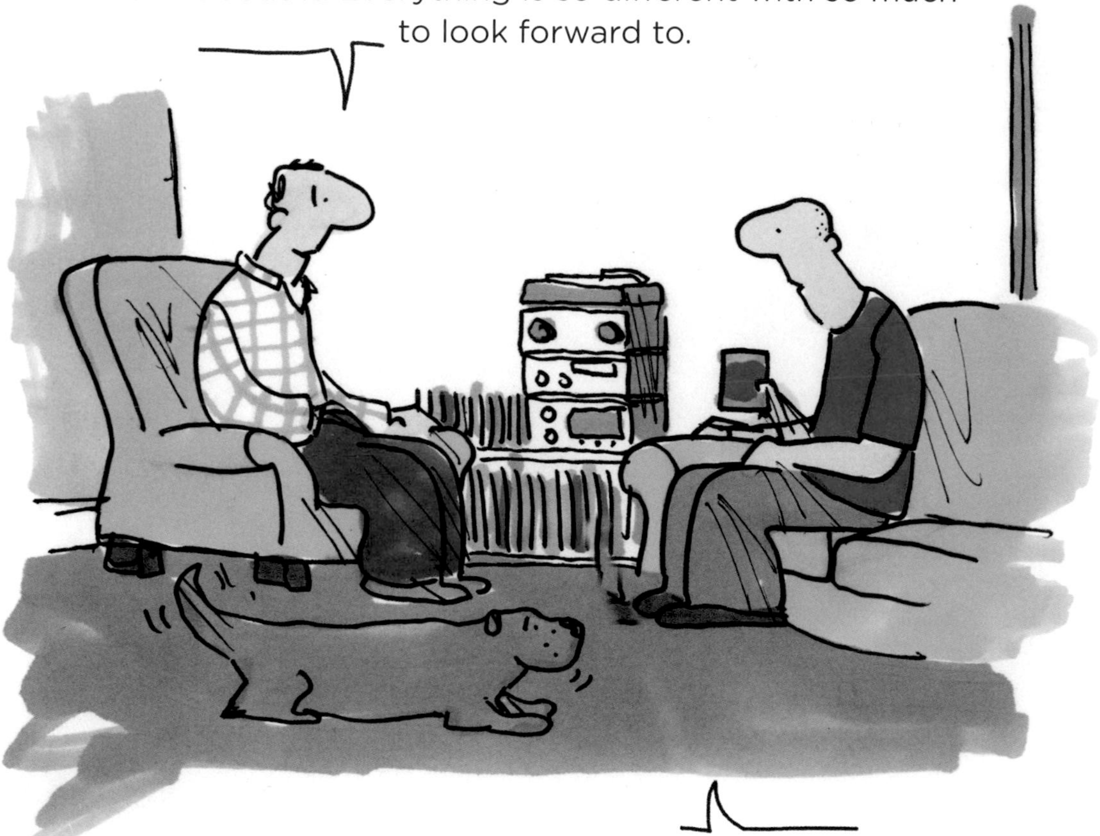
Wow, what a bloody journey... and we're still here to talk about it. Everything is so different with so much to look forward to.
Yes, I know. I owe so much to so many people. But I do know I can't take things for granted... I can't slip up again. I must always remember I'm an addict.

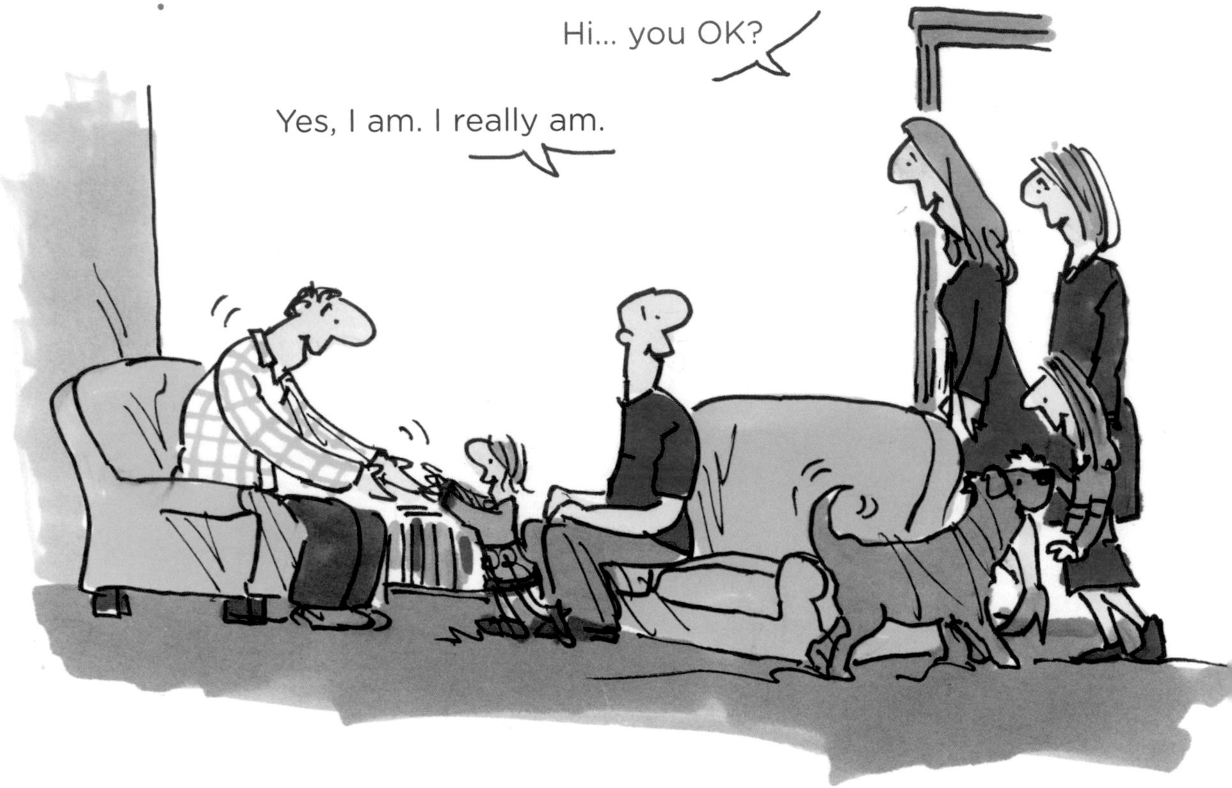
Hi... you OK?
Yes, I am. I really am.

shay rowan photography

If you are concerned about yourself, or about someone you know who may have problems with addiction, it is important to seek advice. There are national organisations who may have local services for the person with addiction and their family members, and who can provide you with practical, emotional and signposting support.

These are just some of the organisations to offer advice:

FRANK	www.talktofrank.org.uk
Narcotics Anonymous	ukna.org
NHS Choices	www.nhs.uk/Livewell/drugs/Pages/Drugtreatment.aspx
Adfam – Families, Drugs and Alcohol	www.adfam.org.uk
Families Anonymous	famanon.org.uk
Action on Addiction	www.actiononaddiction.org.uk
Red Rose Recovery	www.redroserecovery.org.uk
Moodswings	www.moodswings.org.uk